THE CAFE BRENDA COOKBOOK

CAFE BRENDA, the restaurant home of these sinfully healthy, contemporary recipes, can be found in the heart of the historic Minneapolis warehouse district at 300 North First Avenue, Minneapolis, MN 55401.

Additional information may be found at www.cafebrenda.com or by calling the restaurant at (612) 342-9230.

The Twenty-fifth Anniversary Edition

THE CAFE BRENDA COOKBOOK

Seafood and Vegetarian Cuisine

BRENDA LANGTON AND MARGARET STUART

University of Minnesota Press
Minneapolis • London

Originally published by Voyageur Press, 1992
First University of Minnesota Press edition, 2004

Published by the University of Minnesota Press
111 Third Avenue South, Suite 290
Minneapolis, MN 55401-2520
http://www.upress.umn.edu

Library of Congress Cataloging-in-Publication Data

Langton, Brenda, 1957–
    The Cafe Brenda cookbook : seafood and vegetarian cuisine, the twenty-fifth anniversary edition / Brenda Langton and Margaret Stuart.— 1st University of Minnesota Press ed.
        p.   cm.
    Includes index.
    ISBN 0-8166-4439-X (pb. : alk. paper)
    1. Vegetarian cookery.   2. Cookery (Seafood)   3. Cafe Brenda (Minneapolis, Minn.)   I. Stuart, Margaret, 1956–   II. Title.
    TX837.L24 2004
    641.6'92—dc22

                                                                                                2004011773

Printed in the United States of America on acid-free paper

The University of Minnesota is an equal-opportunity educator and employer.

12 11 10 09 08 07 06 05 04   10 9 8 7 6 5 4 3 2 1

To our mothers, Mary Langton & Mary Grace Scher

CONTENTS

Vegetable Entrees   149

Carrot-Walnut-Cheese Loaf with Parsnip-Orange Sauce
Black Bean–Vegetable Chili
Burgundy Mushroom Stew with Garlic Croutons
Curried Chickpea and Vegetable Stew with Couscous
Thai-Style Vegetable and Tofu Stew
Greek Moussaka
Spinach, Zucchini, and Fresh Herb Gratin
Vegetable Terrine Served on a Bed of Linguini
Sautéed Polenta with Stewed Pinto Beans or Fresh Tomato Sauce
Eggplant, Roasted Walnut, and Asparagus Stir-Fry with Udon Noodles
Winter Vegetable Pie
Butternut Squash and Vegetable Gratin Topped with Roasted Walnuts
    and Gruyère Cheese
Millet-Almond Loaf
Vietnamese Warm Tempeh Salad
North African Couscous-Vegetable Pilaf with Harissa Sauce
Shepherd's Pie
Baked, Stuffed Squash with Leek-Orange Sauce

CROQUETTES   187

Buckwheat-Potato with Ginger-Mushroom Sauce
Chickpea-Vegetable with Tahini-Vegetable Sauce
Couscous-Almond with Orange-Shallot Sauce
Basmati Rice, Red Bean, and Vegetable with Salsa
Brown Rice, Almond, and Vegetable with Roasted Onion–Miso Sauce
Roasted Eggplant Patties with Tomato-Basil Sauce
Butternut Squash, Cheese, and Walnut
Tofu, Vegetable, and Peanut with Sweet and Sour Sauce
Wild Rice, Vegetable, and Pecan with Wild Mushroom Cream Sauce
Tempeh-Potato with Spicy Peanut Sambal
Vegetable Pancakes

ACKNOWLEDGMENTS

We would like to thank all of you who have helped make this book become reality. Our cooking style and philosophy have developed over many years through the restaurant and our relationships with cooks, customers, and friends.

Many thanks to all of the staff at both Cafe Kardamena and Cafe Brenda. You have been an inspiration for many of these recipes. Thank you for all your hard work in making Cafe Brenda succeed.

We would like to thank the Scher family for all of their support, especially Sam and Byron for their patience. And thanks to Deanne Levander-Larson for her great technical help and all of our friends who have encouraged us along the way.

INTRODUCTION

In the Twin Cities, where lifestyles are geared toward being healthy and eating good food, is Cafe Brenda, a natural foods restaurant that features fresh seafood and vegetarian cuisine. Intertwining ethnic and American foods, we have created a modern style that uses fresh, unprocessed natural foods and a small amount of dairy products, allowing for low-fat, delicious food. We think of our food as comforting and rejuvenating because it's food that is nutritious, tastes good while you're eating it, and feels good hours after you've eaten it.

We have been a leader in this style of cooking that in recent years has been emerging nationally as important for our health. Nutrition experts now agree that the typical American diet is not the diet for our future—that is, if we want to feel good and be healthy. New knowledge about the benefits of whole grains, beans, fruits, and vegetables as well as the dangers of eating foods high in fat, salt, and sugar are now reflected in a revised basic food group chart. It comes as no surprise that meat and dairy are cut back more than ever. This is exciting, because we believe strongly in eating seafood and vegetarian foods; but for many of us, the change comes as a challenge because the focus of most meals is meat. In this book are many recipes to help make this transition or to expand one's repertoire of meals.

In 1976, when I was twenty, I opened my first restaurant, Cafe Kardamena in St. Paul. The restaurant became my school. Experimenting with exotic foods newly available on the market, I created original dishes, often borrowing techniques from traditional Asian, Mediterranean, Latin, and American cooking. We began Cafe Kardamena cooking in a style that was simple vegetarian cuisine, relying heavily on dairy products. But back then, healthful ingredients took precedence over flavor, and we assembled our dishes in a slapdash manner. Eventually, I learned that flavor need not be sacrificed to nutrition and that careful presentation added to the pleasure of a meal. Eventually, we redefined our recipes into lighter, healthier, and more elegant foods, thus starting a new cooking trend that led us into the 1990s.

Included in this book are many of our most-requested dishes from the past ten years, from appetizers such as Miso & Herb Pâté to our renowned vegetarian croquettes, from savory soups and stews to Poached Rainbow Trout with Fresh Berry Vinaigrette. *The Cafe Brenda Cookbook* tempts you with "sinfully healthy" desserts, sweetened with only natural sugars and containing reduced amounts of dairy products, such as Chocolate Carrot Cake with Chocolate Cream Cheese Frosting, Apple-Cranberry Pie, and Almond-Hazelnut Tart with Fruit Glaze. These recipes are for everyday meals as well as festive occasions and are presented in an easy-to-follow manner. We hope you come to believe, as we do, that our kitchens are the hearts of our homes. Be happy and relaxed in them, and enjoy preparing your food as well as eating it.

BRENDA LANGTON, CAFE BRENDA

APPETIZERS & SALADS

Warm Wisconsin Chèvre Balls Rolled in Roasted Hazelnuts on
a Bed of Greens in Citrus Vinaigrette   20

Japanese Soba Noodle Salad with
Spicy Tahini-Ginger Dressing   22

Broiled Eggplant with Orange-Miso Glaze   25

Miso & Herb Pâté   26

Baked, Stuffed Mussels   27

Smoked Trout or Salmon Mousse   29

Grilled Tofu, Green Onion, Sweet Pepper, & Mushroom
Brochettes in Japanese Marinade   30

Roasted Tomatillo Salsa & Cheese Quesadillas   32

White Bean & Fennel Salad   34

Scallop Ceviche   35

Crab Salad in a Tarragon-Citrus Mayonnaise
with Avocado Slices   36

Cranberry-Fruit Salad   38

Cucumber-Orange Salad   39

Warm Wisconsin Chèvre Balls Rolled in Roasted Hazelnuts on a Bed of Greens in Citrus Vinaigrette

We use Wisconsin goat cheese because of its mild flavor and freshness: However, if you have a favorite chèvre, that would work as well. We often vary the nuts from hazelnuts to walnuts, pecans, or black and white sesame seeds. This salad is best prepared in individual portions, just before serving.

> ½ cup finely chopped, roasted hazelnuts
> 6 ounces chèvre
> assorted greens: spinach, watercress, lettuce, etc.
> 2 apples or pears, sliced
> fresh strawberries, raspberries, or grape clusters (optional)

☐ Place the finely chopped, roasted hazelnuts in a flat bowl.

☐ Divide the cheese into 4 equal pieces. Roll the cheese into balls. Form 2-inch wide rounds by flattening the balls with the palm of your hand. Roll these in the chopped nuts. Set the cheese rounds aside, and prepare the vinaigrette (recipe below).

☐ Wash and dry greens, and tear. When you are ready to serve the salad, toss the greens in enough vinaigrette to lightly coat. Divide the greens onto 4 plates.

☐ Place the chèvre balls in a dry, hot skillet over low heat. Cook for 2 to 3 minutes. Do not flip them. Place the cheese on top of the greens, and arrange the fruit around it. Serve immediately. Serves 4.

CITRUS VINAIGRETTE

2 tablespoons lemon or lime juice
¼ cup grapefruit or orange juice
½ cup walnut, hazelnut, or safflower oil (or a combination)
1 teaspoon fresh herbs: thyme, basil, or marjoram
cracked pepper
salt to taste
1 shallot, minced

☐ Combine all of the vinaigrette ingredients, and whisk together until well mixed. This makes more than you will need for the chèvre recipe. When refrigerated, it will keep for up to a week and is wonderful on any green salad.

ROASTING NUTS

Roasting nuts brings out their flavor. To roast nuts, place them on a cookie sheet and roast them in a preheated 350° oven for approximately 10 minutes. Nuts that have been sliced or chopped may roast a little faster, so check them after 5 minutes and remove them just as they start to color. Cool roasted nuts before you grind them.

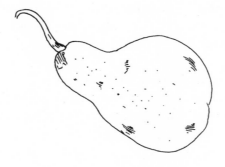

Japanese Soba Noodle Salad with Spicy Tahini-Ginger Dressing

This is a long-time favorite at the restaurant. We serve this both as an entree and as an appetizer. It is a nice, simple meal for summer and is always a good first course. The sauce and vinaigrette can be prepared in advance, making this a fast and easy meal. We've listed the 4 steps here, and it's all put together at the end of the recipe.

SOBA

½ pound soba noodles

☐ Cook soba noodles in boiling water until al dente, approximately 5 to 8 minutes. Rinse and chill.

SPICY TAHINI-GINGER DRESSING

1 teaspoon chili paste
¼ cup peeled and thinly sliced fresh ginger root
3 to 4 cloves garlic, peeled
¼ cup rice vinegar
¼ cup soy sauce or tamari
1½ tablespoons honey
½ cup plus 1 tablespoon tahini
½ cup water
dash of salt

☐ Purée all sauce ingredients in a blender until smooth.
☐ Push the mixture through a fine wire mesh to strain out ginger fibers. Makes approximately 2 cups, enough for 8 entrées, and will keep for 2 weeks if kept refrigerated.

TOASTED SESAME VINAIGRETTE

⅓ cup rice vinegar
¼ cup sunflower or vegetable oil
1 tablespoon toasted sesame oil
1 tablespoon toasted sesame seeds (see instructions on page 78)
½ tablespoon soy sauce
½ tablespoon honey
pinch of cayenne pepper
pinch of salt

☐ Whisk all of the vinaigrette ingredients together.
☐ This vinaigrette works with any green salad. It is also used for the Vietnamese Warm Tempeh Salad (page 178).

SALAD

1 head of lettuce
1 cup blanched pea pods or green beans
1 cup blanched, julienned carrots
1 cucumber, sliced
2 tomatoes, cut in wedges
½ bunch scallions, sliced on the diagonal

SOBA SALAD PRESENTATION

☐ To blanch the vegetables: Bring a small pot of water to boil. Drop in the green beans and carrots for 2 to 3 minutes, and the pea pods in for 30 seconds. Rinse under very cold water immediately.
☐ When you're ready to serve the salad, clean and tear lettuce. In a large bowl, toss lettuce in vinaigrette. Set aside. Toss soba noodles in tahini sauce. On a large platter or individual plates, lay a bed of the dressed lettuce. Mound the dressed soba noodles in the middle. Arrange the vegetables around the noodles and top with the slivered scallions. This makes enough for 6 to 8 appetizers or 3 entrées.

SOBA NOODLES

Soba noodles are thin, flat noodles made with buckwheat flour. There are different varieties available; the most common are those made with 40 percent buckwheat flour and 60 percent wheat flour. You can also find soba noodles make with 100 percent buckwheat and others that have herbs or seaweed added as flavorings. Look for soba noodles at Asian food markets, natural food stores and co-ops, or in the natural foods section of grocery stores.

Broiled Eggplant with Orange-Miso Glaze

Eggplant topped with a bit of this glaze strikes the perfect balance! We like to serve this with a small portion of Japanese somen or soba noodles topped with slivered green onions. Try arranging orange slices on the plate as a colorful garnish. The glaze will last for 2 weeks if kept refrigerated.

2 tablespoons orange juice concentrate
2-inch piece of fresh ginger root, juiced (see instructions on
*   page 113)*
2 tablespoons mirin
3 tablespoons white or light miso
1 medium eggplant or 3 small Japanese eggplants
vegetable oil

☐ Combine orange juice, ginger juice, mirin, and miso in a small bowl. Stir until smooth, and set aside.
☐ Diagonally slice eggplant into ¼-inch round or oval slices. Place eggplant slices on an oiled sheet pan. Brush tops lightly with vegetable oil. Place eggplant slices in a 450° oven and bake until lightly brown (approximately 15 to 20 minutes).
☐ Take out of oven and spoon a coating of miso sauce onto each slice. Return to oven and bake about 5 minutes until golden brown, or place briefly under broiler. Serves 4 to 6.

MIRIN

Mirin is a sweet cooking wine made from fermented sweet rice. It is often the secret ingredient in traditional Japanese cooking. Mirin adds depth of flavor to sauteed vegetables, fresh noodles, sauces, teriyaki, and seafood dishes. It is also used in fish and vegetable glazes.

Traditional mirin has no sugar added. It can be hard to find and is expensive, but a bottle goes a long way. Look for it in natural or Asian food stores. Cooking sake can be used in place of mirin, and is available in liquor stores.

Miso and Herb Pâté

This pâté has been a mainstay on our appetizer menu for the past 6 years and is definitely one of our most requested recipes. It's best served at room temperature with an assortment of fresh vegetables and Homemade Croutons. This is a great choice for large crowds: It's healthy, delicious, and easy to double. Experiment with different misos, because they vary in strength. Yellow miso also works well in this recipe.

1½ cups tahini
1 teaspoon garlic salt or crushed garlic
½ tablespoon dried basil
1½ tablespoons chopped fresh parsley
2 tablespoons red miso
2 tablespoons white miso
2 tablespoons chopped scallions (optional)
½ to ¾ cup water

☐ In a heavy skillet, roast the tahini over medium-high heat, stirring constantly for about 5 minutes. Tahini will turn a golden brown and stick to the pan when it is done. Set it aside in a mixing bowl to cool for about 30 minutes.

☐ When the tahini is room temperature, add garlic or garlic salt, basil, parsley, miso, and scallions. Mix well. An electric mixer or food processor will give the best texture, but you can get a good result stirring vigorously by hand.

☐ Add the water in small amounts, slowly incorporating it until the mixture is smooth and creamy. Tahini varies in its thickness and oil content. If the tahini you have is very thick, use more water as needed. Makes 2 cups.

HOMEMADE CROUTONS
Thinly slice French bread ¼ inch thick. Place the slices on a sheet pan and lightly brush the tops with olive oil. To make garlic croutons, add 4 cloves of minced garlic to the olive oil before brushing on the bread. Bake the bread for 12 to 15 minutes at 425° or until crispy.

Baked, Stuffed Mussels

New Zealand green lip mussels are my favorite—they make a beautiful hors d'oeuvre. You can prepare Baked, Stuffed Mussels ahead of time, because they are easily warmed up in the oven before they are served. We suggest serving 4 to 6 mussels per person for an appetizer. This recipe should make enough stuffing for 32 mussels. Mussels are seasonal—avoid them in the summer months.

24 to 32 mussels
¾ to 1 cup white wine
3 tablespoons olive oil
1 tablespoon minced garlic
1 cup bread crumbs
⅓ cup finely grated Parmesan cheese
1 tablespoon chopped fresh herbs, such as basil, oregano,
  marjoram, or thyme (try a combination or choose just
  one)
1 to 2 tablespoons chopped fresh parsley
2 tablespoons lemon juice
salt and pepper to taste
lemon slices for garnish

☐ Rinse the mussels and pull off any attached beards. Discard any broken or dead mussels. (Open, alive mussels will pull their shells together when firmly tapped.)

☐ In a soup pot, bring the wine to a boil. Place the mussels in the pan. Do not crowd them more than 2 deep. (If all the mussels do not fit, steam them in batches, reusing the wine.) Cover immediately and steam them at high heat for 3 to 4 minutes. The mussels are done when they are steamed open and their meat is pulled together on the inside.

☐ Remove the mussels from the heat and pour into a strainer, discarding the wine. Cool the mussels for a few minutes, and then break off and discard the shells that do not hold the mussel. Detach the mussel from the shell, and then place the mussel back in the shell before stuffing, making eating much easier. You will need only 1 shell per mussel for stuffing.

☐ While the mussels are cooling, briefly sauté the garlic in olive oil in a small skillet, being careful not to burn it.

☐ In a separate bowl, combine bread crumbs, Parmesan, herbs, parsley, lemon juice, and salt and pepper. Add the bread crumb mixture to the garlic and olive oil, and mix well.

☐ Cover each mussel with enough stuffing mixture to form a little mound. Form and press the stuffing with your fingers to hold it together.

☐ You can prepare these in advance up to this point. Refrigerate well covered. Before broiling, bring the mussels to room temperature, which should take about 20 to 30 minutes.

☐ Place mussels on a broiler pan and broil for approximately 3 minutes, browning lightly. Do not overcook or the mussels will dry out quickly. Garnish with lemon slices. Serve immediately. Serves 4 to 6.

Smoked Trout or Salmon Mousse

A fantastic trout farm in Star Prairie, Wisconsin, often supplies us with delicious smoked trout. This is one way we use it. This mousse is delicate but easy to make and can be prepared hours before you need it. It is pretty when piped out of a pastry bag into ramekins or served in a bowl garnished with freshly chopped parsley or herbs. This recipe works with most smoked fish.

1½ cups cleaned, smoked trout or salmon
½ cup cream cheese or Neufchâtel
2 tablespoons half and half
juice of ½ lemon
1 tablespoon chopped fresh herbs, such as basil, marjoram, or
  chives (use one or a combination)
black pepper to taste
⅔ cup heavy cream
assorted breads, crackers, or fresh vegetables

☐ Grind the fish, using a food grinder or a food processor.
☐ Combine fish, cream cheese, and half and half in food processor or with a mixer until smooth and creamy. Add lemon juice, herbs, and pepper. Blend until well mixed.
☐ Whip cream in a separate bowl until stiff. Place fish mixture in a bowl, and fold in whipped cream. Serve with bread, crackers, or vegetables. Makes 2 cups.

Grilled Tofu, Green Onion, Sweet Pepper, and Mushroom Brochettes in Japanese Marinade

These brochettes, or kabobs, are a good first course when you have the grill out for dinner. They are also easily cooked in the broiler. We often serve kabobs as an entrée: Adding more vegetables and serving with rice and a salad makes the kabobs a complete meal. When available, use fresh wild mushrooms instead of or in addition to the button mushrooms and add a special touch to your meal.

JAPANESE MARINADE

1 tablespoon ginger juice (see instructions on page 113)
2 tablespoons white miso
4 tablespoons barley malt
1 tablespoon tamari
1 tablespoon rice vinegar
1 tablespoon toasted sesame oil
cayenne or chili paste to taste
⅛ teaspoon salt

☐ Mix all ingredients together. Marinade is sufficient quantity for 8 to 10 small kabobs.

GRILLED TOFU, GREEN ONION, SWEET PEPPER, AND MUSHROOM BROCHETTES

½ pound firm tofu, rinsed and cut into 16 squares
16 mushrooms (fresh shiitake mushrooms are wonderful if available)
2 bunches of green onion, cut into 16 pieces
1 red bell pepper, cut into 1- to 2-inch cubes

☐ On bamboo skewers, alternate 2 pieces each of tofu, mushroom, onion, and pepper. Dip or brush each kabob generously with the marinade and place in a pan to marinate for 30 minutes to 2 hours.

☐ Place the skewers on tin foil on the grill or in the broiler, turning the kabobs as they brown until cooked on all sides, approximately 10 minutes. Makes 8 small kabobs.

TOFU

Tofu is made from soy milk, which is then curdled in a process similar to how cheese is made using nigari, a natural coagulant extracted from seawater, instead of rennet. When comparing equal amounts of tofu and dairy milk, you'll find that tofu contains more calcium. It is high in protein, its fat is unsaturated, and it is entirely free of cholesterol.

Tofu comes in 3 forms: soft, medium, and firm. Tofu is bland by itself, but it absorbs other flavors well when cooked. It can take on many different textures, depending on your cooking method. If marinated and baked ahead of time, tofu holds up beautifully in stews and stir fries. Soft tofu, with its creamy texture, is best used in sauces, soups, and salad dressings.

Sometimes it is best to press soft tofu, extracting extra liquid and allowing it to be firm and easier to work with. To press the tofu, cut the tofu in half lengthwise, and place each half on a towel. Cover the tofu with a plate and place a weight on the plate (a jar filled with water, or a can of beans, anything to press the liquid out). Leave the weight on for about 20 to 30 minutes. Firm tofu does not need to be pressed.

Roasted Tomatillo Salsa and Cheese Quesadillas

Quesadillas are easy to prepare for a large group. Everyone seems to love them, including children! This recipe is very versatile. The endless variety of peppers—fresh, dried, and smoked— offer unlimited flavor combinations. Make them as spicy as you like, or leave out the peppers for a milder version. Eggplant or tomatoes are good substitutes for the tomatilloes.

½ pound tomatilloes
1 green bell pepper
1 medium onion
1 head of garlic
1 jalapeño pepper
salt to taste
lime juice (optional)
12 8-inch flour tortillas
½ pound mild melting cheese (Monterey jack, mild cheddar,
    or Muenster), grated
1 avocado
fresh cilantro
sour cream

☐ To roast the tomatilloes, peppers, and onions, preheat oven to 400°. Peel paper skin off tomatilloes and wash them well. Cut green pepper in half and remove seeds. Cut onion in half, leaving skin on.

☐ Place tomatilloes, pepper halves, onion halves, whole bulb of garlic, and whole jalapeño on an oiled cookie sheet. Place sheet in oven, and roast until pepper skin blisters, approximately 25 minutes. Check vegetables while roasting, turning them if necessary so they don't burn. Remove from oven.

☐ Place green and jalapeño peppers in a paper bag or under a bowl to sweat for approximately 20 minutes (this will make skins easier to peel). Peel and seed peppers. Peel onions when cool enough to handle.

☐ Cut ½ inch off the top of the garlic bulb with a sharp knife. Hold on to the base of the bulb, and squeeze the roasted garlic pulp into the bowl of a food processor or blender. Add peppers, onions, and tomatilloes, and purée. Add salt to taste. Tomatilloes vary in tartness, so add lime juice as desired.

☐ Place a heaping tablespoon of salsa on one side of a tortilla. Top with some grated cheese and fold tortilla over. Repeat with rest of tortillas.

☐ Place tortillas on a dry cookie sheet. Bake in a 400° oven for 3 to 4 minutes. Slice into wedges and serve with sliced avocado, fresh cilantro, and sour cream.

☐ Makes 6 to 8 servings.

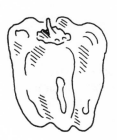

White Bean and Fennel Salad

This salad can be served in a number of ways: as an appetizer with olives and some good hard cheese, or assembled with a couple of other salads as an entrée. We also like to serve it with the Sautéed Halibut with Three Sauces (page 138).

1½ cups white beans
6 cups water
1 tablespoon star anise
1 teaspoon peppercorns
3 bay leaves
1 medium head of garlic, roasted (see instructions on page 201)
4 tablespoons olive oil
1 tablespoon white wine vinegar
juice of 1 lemon
½ teaspoon salt
fresh ground pepper to taste
2 tablespoons chopped fresh parsley
1 cup fennel bulb, thinly sliced
½ cup diced red onion
½ cup diced, blanched carrots
lettuce leaves
sliced tomatoes and black olives for garnish

☐ Place white beans in a soup pot with 6 cups water with anise, peppercorns, and bay leaves. Bring to a boil. Turn down heat and simmer, covered, for approximately 1½ hours, or until tender.

☐ Drain, and discard anise, peppercorns, and bay leaves. Rinse beans in cold water.

☐ Cut ½ inch off the top of the head of roasted garlic. Hold onto the base of the garlic, and squeeze the pulp into a bowl. Add olive oil, vinegar, lemon juice, salt, pepper, and parsley to the garlic and whisk together.

☐ To blanch the carrots: Bring a small pot of water to boil. Drop the carrots in for 2 to 3 minutes, and rinse them immediately with very cold water.

☐ Combine beans with fennel, red onion, and carrot. Pour dressing over the salad and stir gently until well coated.

☐ Serve on a leaf of lettuce and garnish with sliced tomatoes and black olives. Makes 4 to 6 servings.

Scallop Ceviche

Ceviche is a great appetizer because you can prepare it well in advance, even the night before serving it. We also like to serve it as a main course with black beans, flour tortillas, and sweet corn.

> 1 pound fresh sea or bay scallops
> ½ cup fresh lime juice
> 1½ teaspoons minced garlic
> 2 tablespoons minced fresh cilantro
> salt to taste
> 1 medium jalapeño, minced
> 1 bunch scallions, diced small
> 1 medium tomato, minced
> shredded lettuce
> flour tortillas
> avocado, lime, and fresh cilantro for garnish

☐ Rinse the scallops and remove the tough side muscles with a paring knife. Slice sea scallops about ¼ inch thick. Leave bay scallops whole.

☐ Combine all the ingredients except garnishes in a bowl, mix gently, and let marinate in the refrigerator for at least 4 hours.

☐ Serve on a bed of shredded lettuce with garnish of sliced avocado, lime wedges, fresh cilantro sprigs, and warm flour tortillas on the side. Serves 6.

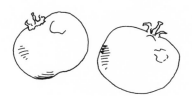

Crab Salad in a Tarragon-Citrus Mayonnaise with Avocado Slices

This is a deluxe salad. When you can find fresh crabmeat, it's a real treat. A pound of crabmeat does go a long way. We serve this with crackers or Homemade Croutons (recipe page 26).

TARRAGON-CITRUS MAYONNAISE

1 egg yolk
½ tablespoon lime juice
½ teaspoon salt
1 cup vegetable oil (use a good quality canola oil; sunflower
    or safflower is also good)
1 tablespoon grapefruit or orange juice
1 teaspoon chopped fresh tarragon
3 tablespoons chopped chives
⅛ teaspoon pepper

☐ Drop the egg yolk into a bowl, add the lime juice and salt, and beat or whisk vigorously. Slowly add the oil in a light stream until mixture begins to thicken.
☐ Continue to beat the mayonnaise until all the oil is incorporated. Add the grapefruit or orange juice, tarragon, chives, and pepper. Whisk together.

CRAB SALAD

1 pound crabmeat
3 avocados
3 oranges
1 to 2 grapefruit
lettuce or wild greens

☐ Carefully clean the crabmeat, picking out any shell pieces. Mix the crabmeat and mayonnaise together.

☐ Slice avocados. Peel and segment the oranges and grapefruit, cleaning each until all membranes are gone.

☐ Place lettuce or greens on individual salad plates. Fan out the sliced avocado, using half of the avocado for each serving. Place the crab salad at the base of the avocado and place the fruit segments around it. Serves 6.

Cranberry-Fruit Salad

This salad complements several of our croquettes: Buckwheat-Potato (page 188), Brown Rice, Almond, and Vegetable (page 196), and Wild Rice, Vegetable, and Pecan (page 204). It also works well with some of the vegetarian entrées such as the Millet-Almond Loaf (page 176) or Winter Vegetable Pie (page 173). Its semisweet and tart fruits are refreshing, and the grapes and orange segments make it colorful and festive. Cranberry-Fruit Salad keeps up to a week.

> 1 12-ounce package cranberries
> ½ cup pear or apple juice
> ¼ teaspoon cinnamon
> ⅓ cup honey
> 1 cup grapes
> ½ to 1 cup orange segments
> 1 pear or apple, diced

☐ In a saucepan, bring the berries, juice, cinnamon, and honey to a boil over medium heat. Stir occasionally. Let the sauce boil rapidly for about 1 minute until most of the berries pop.
☐ Pour sauce into a bowl and cool.
☐ Cut up all the fruit and mix into the cooled berries. Serve chilled.

Cucumber-Orange Salad

This simple salad is a light and fresh accompaniment to a meal. Because there's no oil in the dressing, Cucumber-Orange Salad goes well with a meal that is already rich.

1 cucumber
2 oranges (or 1 orange and 1 grapefruit)
½ medium red onion, peeled and sliced thin
2 tablespoons rice vinegar
salt to taste

☐ Peel cucumber, and cut in half lengthwise. Scoop out the seeds, and slice very thin. Peel the fruit and section it, cutting the sections away from the membrane. Combine the fruit, cucumber, red onion, and vinegar. Salt lightly.

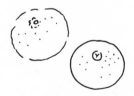

SOUPS

Vegetable Stock

A good stock is essential for a full-flavored soup. Some soups can be made with water instead of stock, but stock always adds to the flavor.

Making Vegetable Stock does not take up much time. It can simmer while you prepare the soup vegetables; it can also be made ahead of time and refrigerated or frozen until you are ready for it.

We do not have one all-purpose stock recipe because our stock varies with the kind of soup we are making and what we have on hand. Certain vegetables are basic to every stock: onion, celery, carrots, and herbs. Our recipe includes these and more, and it lists some suggestions for variations. Some of our soup recipes list specific stock additions; other recipes simply call for soup stock. Use this basic recipe, adjusting it to fit what you have in your kitchen.

> *1 tablespoon vegetable oil*
> *1 medium onion, chopped*
> *2 carrots, chopped (carrots need not be peeled)*
> *2 stalks celery, chopped (celery leaves are nice too)*
> *2 to 3 cloves garlic, smashed*
> *6 to 8 whole sprigs fresh parsley*
> *2 tablespoons chopped fresh herbs, such as bay leaves, thyme,*
> > *or marjoram (or 2 teaspoons dried herbs)*
> *10 to 12 peppercorns*
> *6 to 8 cups water*

☐ Wash vegetables and chop well.

☐ Heat vegetable oil in a soup pot and sauté the onion, carrot, and celery for 3 to 5 minutes. When you sauté the vegetables you help bring out their flavors, but skip this step if you want to reduce the stock's fat content.

☐ Add the rest of the ingredients, and bring to a boil. Reduce the heat, and simmer, covered, for 20 to 30 minutes.

☐ Remove from the heat and strain the vegetables and herbs from the liquid, using a colander and a large measuring cup or saucepan. Do not let unstrained stock sit: Some vegetables may turn bitter if they sit for any length of time.

OPTIONAL INGREDIENTS FOR STOCK

Winter squash: Cut up the squash for your soup before you make the stock, and use the peels and seeds in your stock. Both the peels and seeds add a lot of flavor and body to stock, and are especially good in soups containing winter squash. See instructions for peeling winter squash on page 175.

Summer squash: Stock is a good use for summer squash when you have mountains of it from the garden. It adds a delicate flavor, a nice addition to summer soups.

Parsnip: If you have unwaxed parsnips from the market or your garden, use the peelings and core for a slightly sweet flavor.

Broccoli stems: Save broccoli stems and peel them. Chop and add for an earthy taste.

Leeks: Use leeks instead of or in addition to onions. Leeks are milder and sweeter than onions. Most recipes calling for leeks ask for the white bulbous end only. Save the leaves for soup stock. One cup of chopped leaves is enough for 6 cups of stock.

Mushrooms: Wild mushrooms, although expensive, add a tremendous amount of flavor. Just a few stems or broken pieces will go a long way. Dried mushrooms—*shiitake, porcini,* and morels—have unique, woodsy flavors. Add them to any stock being used for stews and soups that contain mushrooms. Domestic button mushrooms will not add as much flavor.

Green beans: We always seem to have some tough, overgrown beans that are not suitable for serving. These add a lot of flavor to summer stocks.

Corn cobs: Corn cobs are called for in the Corn Chowder recipe in which the corn is sliced off, leaving cobs full of sweet corn "milk." Add these cobs to the stock pot for a great corn flavor. Corn cobs may be used in the stock for other soups as well; just remember that they result in a slightly milky liquid that you may not want to use for a clear soup.

Bonito fish flakes: Bonito flakes add a mild, smoky, fish flavor to stock. They are often used in Oriental cooking. Add a small amount to stock for a fuller flavor.

Beet-Orange

Beet-Orange Soup is a brilliant red soup that tastes great! Try it as the first course of a cool summer meal. Garnish each serving with a dollop of yogurt or an orange slice.

> 1 tablespoon vegetable oil
> ½ cup chopped onion
> 1-inch piece of ginger root, peeled and cut in half
> 1½ pounds beets (5 medium beets), peeled and sliced
> 1 medium carrot, peeled and sliced
> 2 cups Vegetable Stock (see recipe on page 44)
> 3 ounces orange juice concentrate
> 3 tablespoons white miso
> salt and pepper to taste

☐ In a medium saucepan, sauté onions in vegetable oil until soft. Add beets, ginger, and carrots. Continue to sauté over medium heat for 15 minutes, stirring frequently.

☐ Add Vegetable Stock, and simmer, covered, until beets and carrots are quite tender, approximately 30 to 40 minutes. Remove ginger.

☐ Add miso, orange juice concentrate, and salt and pepper. Pour soup in a blender and purée until smooth. Puréeing is best done in 2 batches, filling the blender only half full to avoid the hot soup forcing the lid off. Allow soup to cool for several hours. Serve chilled. Serves 4 to 6.

Cherry-Lemon

When cherries are in season, this soup is a must! It has a rich, sweet flavor with just a hint of cinnamon. We have found it to be a favorite with children. If you would like to make it without the wine, substitute apple or cherry juice.

> 2 pounds fresh, sweet cherries
> juice of 1 lemon
> 1 cinnamon stick, 2 to 3 inches long
> ⅓ cup honey
> 4 cups water
> 1 cup dry white wine
> 3 egg yolks
> sour cream (optional) for garnish

☐ Wash and pit cherries. Put them in a soup pot with lemon juice, cinnamon stick, honey, and water. Bring to a boil and simmer, covered, 15 to 20 minutes.

☐ Drain cherries, saving liquid. Discard cinnamon stick. Remove about 2 dozen cherries and set aside. Purée remaining cherries in blender.

☐ In a soup pot, combine cherry purée, cherry liquid, and wine. Put on low heat. Whisk in egg yolks. Simmer, uncovered, for 5 minutes, whisking occasionally.

☐ Chill soup well. When serving, put 3 or 4 cherries in each bowl and fill with soup. May be served with a dollop of sour cream. Serves 8.

Cucumber-Dill

This soup is very refreshing. It is great for a hot summer day, and is a good way to use up the abundance of cucumbers in season. Stay away from the big cukes, because they will impart a bitter taste to the soup.

3 tablespoons olive oil
4 medium cucumbers, peeled, seeded, and chopped
4 scallions, chopped
salt and pepper to taste
2 teaspoons chopped fresh dill (or 1 teaspoon dried dill weed)
1 cup water or Vegetable Stock (see recipe on page 44)
¾ cup plain yogurt
chopped scallions, fresh dill, and yogurt for garnish

☐ Sauté cucumbers and scallions in oil until cucumber is tender. Add salt and pepper to taste.
☐ Remove from heat, and purée in blender with dill and stock. Cool to room temperature. Combine with ¾ cup yogurt and adjust seasonings.
☐ Chill for 1 hour or more. Garnish with fresh dill, scallions, or yogurt. Serves 4 to 6.

Fruit

Fruit soup is a simple, refreshing start for a summer meal. Use whatever fruit is in season, and experiment with fruit combinations, juices, herbs, and liqueurs. Try peaches with a little fresh ginger juice or apricots with orange juice. The combinations are endless!

1½ cups apple juice or white grape juice
1 pint of strawberries
2 medium cantaloupes
1 tablespoon chopped fresh mint
1 tablespoon fruit liqueur (kirsch, triple sec, and Grand
    Marnier™ are good choices)
pinch of ground cardamom
raspberry vinegar, or lemon or lime juice, to taste
½ to 1 cup plain yogurt

☐ Clean and cut fruit. Put all ingredients except yogurt into a blender and purée until smooth.
☐ Pour into a large bowl and whisk in yogurt. Serve at room temperature or chilled. Serves 6 to 8.

Melon-Mint

There is nothing like the taste sensation of a really good cantaloupe. When cantaloupe is at its peak, everyone at the market is searching for the perfect melon. As we all know, it's a real disappointment to come home with a bland one. This soup blends that wonderful melon flavor with a hint of mint—a great combination. This is a good first course for a summer brunch.

1 large cantaloupe (approximately 3 pounds)
½ cup white wine
½ cup apple juice
1 tablespoon lemon juice
1 tablespoon chopped fresh mint
½ cup plain yogurt
honey

☐ Cut cantaloupe into chunks and put in a blender with wine, juices, and mint. Blend until smooth.
☐ Pour into a bowl and whisk in yogurt. Taste and adjust seasonings: You may want to add more mint or perhaps a little honey. Serves 4 to 6.

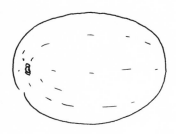

Split Pea–Mint

This soup is very good served either hot or cold, and, when puréed, it has a wonderful creamy texture. With bread and fruit or salad, the cold soup makes a complete and cool meal for the hot summer days. To serve it hot, omit the yogurt and add a few carrots and celery ribs, and top with croutons.

1½ cups dried green split peas, washed well
4 cups water
4 cups water or Vegetable Stock (see recipe on page 44)
1 small onion, sliced
2 cloves garlic, crushed
2 3-inch sprigs of fresh mint
salt to taste
2 carrots, chopped (for hot soup only)
2 celery ribs, chopped (for hot soup only)
2 cups plain yogurt (or 1 cup yogurt and 1 cup sour cream)
yogurt and fresh mint for garnish

☐ Wash the peas, and bring them to a boil for 5 minutes in 4 cups of water. Remove from the heat and drain.

☐ Put peas back in saucepan with 4 more cups of water or stock. Bring to a boil, and add onion, garlic, mint, and salt (if serving the soup hot, add 3 chopped carrots and 2 chopped celery ribs). Reduce heat and simmer, covered, until peas are tender, approximately 45 minutes.

☐ Discard mint, and purée peas and liquid in a blender in small batches. Cool thoroughly. Peas will need about 4 hours to cool.

☐ Before serving, whisk in yogurt. Garnish with a dollop of yogurt and a sprig of mint. Serves 6 to 8.

Barley-Mushroom

Barley is an excellent grain for soup making. It adds a creamy texture to the broth, and it is hearty and warming. Try substituting dried lentils for half of the barley—the combination is wonderful! This soup is just as good the second day as it is the first, but barley tends to absorb liquid as it sits, so if you have leftovers, be prepared to add a little more stock—or eat it as stew.

7 cups Vegetable Stock (see recipe on page 44)
¾ cup pearl barley
4 tablespoons butter or vegetable oil
1 pound mushrooms, washed and sliced
1 medium onion, chopped
3 cloves garlic, minced
1 stalk celery, chopped
1 carrot, diced
salt and freshly ground pepper to taste
½ teaspoon dried thyme
½ teaspoon dried basil
2 tablespoons soy sauce or tamari
¼ cup red wine (optional)

☐ Bring 2 cups of the stock to a boil. Add barley. Bring the stock back to a boil, then reduce the heat and simmer, covered, until the barley is tender, approximately 20 minutes. (If using lentils, cook them with the barley.) Set aside.

☐ Sauté half of the mushrooms in 2 tablespoons butter or oil for 8 to 10 minutes. Purée the mushrooms in the blender with 1 cup of stock and set aside.

☐ Sauté the onions and garlic in remaining butter over medium heat until onions are soft. Add celery and carrot. Sauté until the carrots are tender, about 5 minutes, and then add remaining mushrooms. Continue to sauté until mushrooms are tender, approximately another 5 minutes.

☐ Combine sautéed vegetables with barley, mushroom purée, salt and pepper, herbs, soy sauce or tamari, wine, and remaining 4 cups of stock in a soup pot. Cover and simmer over medium heat for 15 to 20 minutes. Serves 6.

Black Bean

Black Bean soup is an earthy soup with a rich bean flavor. Serve it as a first course with Snapper Caribbean-Style (page 136) or Butternut Squash, Cheese, and Walnut Croquettes (page 200). It is also a great meal in itself with tortillas or Buttermilk Cornbread (page 107) and a salad.

2 cups dried black beans
6 cups water
1 tablespoon vegetable oil
1 onion, diced
4 cloves garlic, chopped
1 stalk celery, diced
2 large carrots, diced
1 teaspoon cumin
¼ teaspoon cayenne
salt to taste
4 cups Vegetable Stock (see recipe on page 44)
3 tomatoes, peeled, seeded, and chopped
2 tablespoons tomato paste
2 tablespoons dry sherry
1 tablespoon tamari or soy sauce
sour cream and fresh cilantro for garnish

☐ Sort through the beans for smalls rocks, and rinse with water to clean. Put the beans in a soup pot with the 6 cups of water. Bring to a boil. Reduce the heat, and simmer, covered, until beans are tender, approximately 1½ hours.

☐ While the beans are cooking, sauté onions and garlic in oil until onions are soft. Add celery, carrots, cumin, cayenne, and salt. Sauté until carrots are tender, about 5 minutes.

☐ Drain beans. Combine beans, stock, and vegetables in a large soup pot. Add tomatoes, tomato paste, sherry, and tamari or soy sauce. Adjust seasonings to taste. Simmer for 20 to 30 minutes.

☐ Before serving, garnish with sour cream and cilantro. Serves 8 to 10.

Chickpea-Pumpkin

Pumpkin soup is a fall favorite of ours. This recipe uses chickpeas and oatmeal for a hearty, rich flavor. Serve this soup with bread and a tabouli salad for a satisfying meal. We suggest serving it as a first course to Walleye Sautéed in Almond Meal (page 125).

1 cup dried chickpeas
4 cups water for soaking
6 cups water for cooking
1 small pumpkin
3 tablespoons vegetable oil
1 medium onion, coarsely chopped
5 cups water or Vegetable Stock (see recipe on page 44, and
*   use the pumpkin peel in stock!)*
1½ teaspoons salt
½ teaspoon dried thyme
¼ cup rolled oats

☐ Soak chickpeas for at least 4 hours (overnight, if possible) in the 4 cups of water.

☐ Pour off and discard the soaking liquid. Combine chickpeas in a soup pot with 6 cups of water. Bring to a boil. Reduce the heat and simmer, covered, over medium heat until tender, approximately 1 to 1½ hours.

☐ Peel the pumpkin (see instructions on page 175), and cut it in half. Clean out the seeds and stringy portion, and cut the flesh into 1-inch pieces. You should have 5 to 6 cups of pumpkin.

☐ In a soup pot, sauté onion in 3 tablespoons vegetable oil until soft. Add pumpkin and sauté for an additional 10 minutes. Add water or stock, salt, thyme, and rolled oats.

☐ Cover pot and simmer over medium heat until pumpkin is tender, approximately 30 minutes. Add beans and continue cooking for another 10 to 15 minutes. As the soup continues to cook, the pumpkin will fall apart into a purée. You may decide to cook it long enough for a creamy soup, or to serve it while the pumpkin is still in chunks. Serves 6.

Corn Chowder

Because so many new corn hybrids have extended the corn season, we have the opportunity to make fresh corn chowder more often than in the past. Nothing can equal the sweet, rich flavor of the "milk" from fresh corn cobs when they are used in the stock. Our version has no cream, but is plenty rich without it.

8 ears sweet corn
2 tablespoons vegetable oil or butter
1 medium onion, chopped
2 medium carrots, diced
2 stalks celery, diced
3 medium potatoes, cubed (should have 3 cups)
5 cups Vegetable Stock (see recipe on page 44)
1 teaspoon salt (or more to taste)
1 teaspoon fresh herbs, chopped (optional)
fresh ground pepper to taste

☐ Use 2 methods to remove kernels from the cob so that you will have different textures. Cut the kernels from 4 of the ears: Starting at the tip of each ear, cut straight down, leaving about ⅛ inch of pulp on the cob.

☐ Scrape the kernels from the remaining 4 ears: With a sharp knife, slice down the center of a row from the tip to the end of the ear. Repeat until you have sliced every row. Lay the corn over a bowl, and scrape the kernels with a knife, pushing the "milk" from the corn. Go around the whole ear, extracting as much of the milk as you can. Use the cobs when making your stock.

☐ Sauté onions in butter or vegetable oil for 3 to 5 minutes. Add carrots and celery and sauté another 5 to 8 minutes or until the vegetables are soft. Add potatoes, cut and scraped corn, and stock. Season with salt, herbs, and fresh ground black pepper to taste. Cover and simmer 20 to 30 minutes.

☐ Remove 2 cups of the soup and purée in a blender. Add the purée back to the soup. The soup is now ready to serve, or may be kept at a low simmer until ready to serve. Serves 6 to 8.

Tomato

Tomatoes and basil straight from the garden turn this often overlooked classic into a unique summer favorite. Serve this soup with a loaf of fresh-baked bread or grilled cheese sandwiches.

6 large fresh tomatoes, peeled, or 1 large can (28 ounces)
   tomatoes
1 tablespoon olive oil
1 medium onion, chopped
1 stalk celery, chopped
1 cup Vegetable Stock (see recipe on page 44)
1 tablespoon chopped fresh basil
½ teaspoon salt
black pepper to taste
½ cup half and half or heavy cream (optional)

☐ To peel tomatoes: Boil 4 to 6 cups water. One by one, drop the tomatoes into boiling water. Leave them for a few minutes, and then take them out and plunge them into a bowl of very cold water. When tomatoes are cool, slip off their peels.

☐ Cut tomatoes in half and squeeze out seeds. Set 1 tomato aside to add to puréed soup at the end for texture.

☐ Chop the remaining tomatoes. You should have 4 cups of chopped tomato.

☐ Sauté onion in olive oil until the onion is translucent. Add celery, and sauté until celery is tender, about 5 minutes.

☐ Combine chopped tomatoes, stock, onion, celery, basil, salt, and pepper in a soup pot. Simmer for 10 minutes. Purée the soup until smooth in a blender in 2 batches.

☐ Return the purée to the soup pot, coarsely chop the 1 remaining tomato, and add it to the soup. For a creamy soup, add ½ cup half and half or heavy cream. Serves 4 to 6.

Curried Lentil and Sweet Potato

This soup is a spicy, rich blend of curry, coconut, and sweet potatoes. Its colors and smells are as rich as its flavors, making this an impressive soup to serve.

> *2 tablespoons vegetable oil*
> *1 large red onion, diced*
> *6 to 7 cloves garlic, minced*
> *¼ cup peeled and minced ginger root*
> *1½ tablespoons curry powder*
> *1 hot chili pepper (dried or fresh), minced*
> *1 cup diced carrots*
> *1 cup diced sweet red bell pepper*
> *5 cups diced sweet potato*
> *1 14-ounce can coconut milk*
> *2 cups dried lentils, washed*
> *8 cups Vegetable Stock (see recipe on page 44)*
> *juice of 1 lime*
> *1 bunch of cilantro, minced*

☐ Sauté red onion, garlic, and ginger in oil for 15 minutes in a large soup pot. Add curry powder, hot pepper, carrots, bell pepper, and sweet potatoes. Sauté another 5 to 10 minutes.
☐ Add coconut milk, lentils, and stock. Simmer, covered, until lentils are done and sweet potatoes are tender, approximately 45 minutes. Add lime juice and cilantro. Serves 6 to 8.

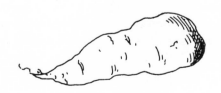

Fennel, Squash, and Sweet Bell Pepper

Fennel is a vegetable that, to our delight, is getting much more recognition these days. It has a distinct anise flavor that combines well with the sweet flavors of squash and leeks. Fennel often has outside ribs that are broken and scarred. Use these as well as the tops for stock, reserving the inner bulb for the soup.

1 small butternut or buttercup squash
1 large leek, sliced into ½-inch pieces
1 apple (optional)
1 bulb fennel
1 large golden or red sweet bell pepper
2 tablespoons vegetable or olive oil
5 cups Vegetable Stock (see recipe on page 44)
1 teaspoon salt
pepper to taste

☐ Peel and seed squash (see instructions on page 175), and cut it into 1-inch cubes; you should have approximately 4 cups. Cut off the green top of the leek and either discard it or save it for the soup stock.

☐ Peel and core the apple, and cut it into 1-inch chunks.

☐ Clean the fennel: Cut off and discard the green tops and discard the outer rib if it is bruised. Cut the remaining fennel into 1-inch pieces—you should have approximately 1½ cups.

☐ Either roast and peel the bell pepper (see instructions in Roasted Tomatillo Salsa and Cheese Quesadillas recipe on page 32), or chop and seed the pepper and sauté it with the leek in a large soup pot in the oil for 3 minutes. Add fennel and sauté 3 more minutes. Add the squash, apple, bell pepper, stock, salt, and pepper.

☐ Bring to a boil, reduce heat, and simmer, covered, for 30 minutes or until squash is well done. Let cool slightly, and purée in a blender in small batches until smooth. Serves 6 to 8.

Ginger-Squash

This rich and creamy soup is often requested at Cafe Brenda in fall and winter. We consider it to be the ultimate "comfort food." You can experiment with the many winter squash varieties. Some are sweeter or richer than others, but they all make great soup.

1 medium butternut or buttercup squash
2 tablespoons vegetable oil
1 medium yellow onion, chopped
3 tablespoons peeled and chopped ginger root
2 large cloves garlic, chopped
4 cups Vegetable Stock (see recipe on page 44)
3 tablespoons yellow or white miso
½ teaspoon salt
¼ teaspoon white pepper
juice of 1 orange
¼ to ½ cup half and half (optional)

☐ Wash the squash well. Peel (see instructions on page 175), and use the peelings in the stock. Chop the squash into 1-inch pieces, discarding the seeds. You should have about 4½ cups chopped squash.

☐ In a large soup kettle, sauté the onion, ginger, and garlic in vegetable oil. When the onion softens, add the squash and sauté for 5 more minutes.

☐ Add stock and cover pot. Simmer over medium heat for 30 to 40 minutes.

☐ Add miso, salt, pepper, and orange juice. Purée soup in a blender in batches, if necessary, until smooth. Add cream. If the soup is too thick, add more soup stock. Serves 4 to 6.

Miso-Vegetable

This recipe is only one variation of a Japanese vegetable soup that has endless combinations. Just remember to keep it quick and simple. Squash always adds richness, but you can create a sure winner with cooked, puréed carrots as well. Another delicious addition is seaweed— *arame* or *wakame* are the best varieties to use. Add bonito fish flakes to the stock for a fuller flavor.

2 to 3 cups winter squash
2 cups Chinese cabbage
1 bunch (6 to 8) scallions
¼ to ½ pound tofu, firm or soft
1½ tablespoons peeled and chopped fresh ginger root
1 tablespoon sesame oil
1 tablespoon vegetable oil
1 medium onion, sliced
4 cloves garlic, minced
5 cups Vegetable Stock (see recipe on page 44)
1½ tablespoons white miso
1½ tablespoons mellow red miso
½ cup water

☐ Peel and cut winter squash into 1-inch cubes (see instructions on page 175). Clean cabbage well, and slice it into ½- to 1-inch strips. Clean scallions, and chop into ½-inch sections.
☐ Rinse tofu and cut into 1-inch cubes. Peel ginger, slice thinly, and chop.
☐ In a soup pot, sauté onion and garlic in sesame and vegetable oils over low heat for 3 minutes. Add squash, and continue to sauté, stirring for 3 more minutes.
☐ Add soup stock, bring to a boil, then reduce the heat and simmer, covered, for approximately 15 minutes or until squash is tender. Add cabbage, scallions, tofu, and ginger. Simmer for 2 to 3 minutes.
☐ In a small bowl, whisk together both the white and red miso and ½ cup water. Add some of the miso-water mixture to the soup. Because miso often varies in flavor and strength, the quantity to add to the soup depends on how strong of a miso taste you desire. Taste the soup and add more miso as needed. Serve immediately; do not let the soup boil. Serves 4 to 6.

MISO

There are many different types of miso. Most common are those made by fermenting soybeans, salt, and a grain—barley, rice, or corn. New and different misos are now being made with other legumes and grains. Miso contains protein, vitamins, and minerals. Its living enzymes aid digestion and strengthen our blood.

White and yellow misos are mild. Red and brown misos have a more intense flavor. Use the mild misos for fish and summer soups; use the red and brown misos in winter foods and when you want something more robust. Miso adds flavor to sauces, soups, croquettes, and spreads.

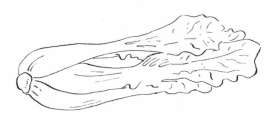

Italian Lentil

This hearty soup can be a meal in itself, especially when served with bread and cheese. We like to use star anise in this soup's stock. The anise adds a bit of Mediterranean flavor.

2 cups lentils
8 cups Vegetable Stock (see recipe on page 44)
1½ teaspoons salt
2 tablespoons olive oil
1 medium onion, chopped
4 cloves garlic, chopped
2 large carrots, peeled and diced
2 stalks celery, chopped
2 cups peeled, seeded, and chopped tomatoes (canned or fresh)
1 teaspoon dry mustard
1 teaspoon dried thyme
fresh ground pepper to taste
2 tablespoons red wine vinegar

☐ Clean lentils, and put them in a large pot. Cover with the stock. Add salt, and bring to a boil. Reduce heat, and simmer, covered, for 30 minutes.

☐ Sauté onion, garlic, carrots, and celery in olive oil until carrots are tender. Add to cooked lentils.

☐ Add tomatoes to lentils. (If using canned tomatoes, add canning liquid.) Add mustard, thyme, and pepper. Continue simmering for approximately 30 minutes, but soup may cook longer at a low simmer.

☐ Add vinegar a few minutes before serving. This soup keeps well and tastes just as good on the second day. Serves 8.

Red Bean, Shiitake Mushroom, and Ginger

This takes a turn from the traditional bean soup. The woodsy wild mushroom and ginger flavors are perfect complements to the red bean. In cool weather, this makes a good first course for the Brown Rice, Almond, and Vegetable Croquettes with Roasted Onion–Miso Sauce (page 196).

2 cups dried red beans
6 cups water for cooking
1 cup water for soaking
½ ounce dried shiitake mushrooms
3 tablespoons vegetable or sesame oil
1 medium onion, diced
2 large carrots, peeled and diced
1 stalk celery, diced
1 large leek, diced
1 sweet red bell pepper, diced
6 to 7 cloves garlic, crushed
¼ cup peeled and finely chopped ginger root
7 cups Vegetable Stock (see recipe on page 44)
4 tablespoons tamari or soy sauce
salt to taste
¼ teaspoon cayenne pepper

☐ Wash red beans and cover them with 6 cups of water. Bring to a boil, and then reduce the heat and simmer, covered, until beans are tender, approximately 1½ hours. (Soaking beans ahead of time reduces the cooking time.)
☐ Soak mushrooms in 1 cup water until completely softened, about 30 minutes, and save soaking water. Remove and discard stems, and slice caps thinly.
☐ Sauté onion in vegetable or sesame oil. When onion is soft, add carrots and celery and sauté for 3 more minutes. Add leek, pepper, garlic, and ginger, and sauté another 3 to 5 minutes.
☐ Combine stock, mushroom water, mushrooms, beans, and sautéed vegetables in a large soup pot. Bring soup to a simmer, uncovered, and cook until soup is heated and flavors combine, approximately 15–20 minutes. Add tamari, salt, and cayenne just before serving. Serves 8 to 10.

Parsnip-Apple

This is a delicate winter soup that can be served plain or made a little richer with cream. We have found that parsnips and oranges also make a good combination. For this variation, omit the apple and add about 3 tablespoons orange juice concentrate to the soup stock.

2 tablespoons butter or vegetable oil
2 medium onions, chopped
3 cloves garlic, chopped
3 cups peeled and chopped parsnips
1 large tart apple, chopped (2 cups)
4½ cups Vegetable Stock (see recipe on page 44)
salt and white pepper to taste
½ to 1 cup half and half or soy milk (optional)

☐ Sauté onions and garlic in butter or oil for 3 to 5 minutes in soup pot. Add parsnips and apple, and sauté for an additional 5 minutes. Add soup stock. Simmer, covered, over low heat for approximately 30 minutes.

☐ Blend until creamy in a blender. Add salt and pepper to taste. Whisk in some half and half, or soy milk if desired, and reheat if necessary. Serves 4 to 6.

Roasted Potato and Garlic

This soup is a very simple yet satisfying meal to make, and it is extra special because of the roasted potatoes and garlic. Roasting vegetables really brings out their flavors. Although it seems like a lot, the garlic, once it is roasted, really has a delicate flavor. Serve the soup as a first course with fish or a vegetable gratin, or serve it as a meal with bread, cheese, and a salad. We like to serve it with Pumpernickel Rye Bread (page 90) and sharp cheddar cheese.

> 6 medium red potatoes
> 1 large onion, roughly chopped
> 2 tablespoons olive oil
> 3 heads of garlic
> 5 cups Vegetable Stock (see recipe on page 44)
> 1 cup half and half (optional)
> 1½ teaspoons salt
> cracked fresh pepper

☐ Peel potatoes, leaving about ⅓ of the peel on. Cut into 1-inch pieces; you should have 6 cups.

☐ Mix potato and onion in a large bowl with the 2 tablespoons olive oil, stirring until well-coated. Spread on a cookie sheet, and bake at 400°.

☐ After approximately 10 minutes, place the whole garlic heads in the oven (directly on the oven shelf or on the cookie sheet if there is room), and roast the potatoes, onions, and garlic for approximately 30 more minutes at 400°.

☐ Remove the potatoes and garlic from the over. When the potatoes are easily pierced with a fork and the garlic is very soft, remove the papery outer skin that covers the garlic head. Cut the top ½ inch off the garlic bulb, hold onto the bottom of the bulb, and squeeze the cooked garlic pulp into a bowl.

☐ Combine potatoes, onions, garlic, soup stock, and half and half in a blender. It seems to work best if done in 2 batches. Blend until slightly chunky, not creamy (be careful not to over purée).

☐ Pour blended potato mixture into a soup pot. Add salt and pepper to taste, and heat until warmed through, being careful not to let it boil. Serves 6 to 8.

Spanish Vegetable–Garbanzo Bean

A spicy-sweet combination of vegetables and spices, this is a popular soup both at the restaurant and at home. Spanish Vegetable–Garbanzo Bean soup is a rich medley of colors and flavors, and it is great to serve all year long.

1 cup dried garbanzo beans
4 cups water for soaking
6 cups water for cooking
3 tablespoons olive oil
2 medium onions, chopped
4 cloves garlic, crushed
2 stalks celery, chopped
4 cups sweet potato, winter squash, or carrot
8 cups Vegetable Stock (see recipe on page 44)
1 tablespoon paprika
2 teaspoons turmeric
2 teaspoons dried basil
2 teaspoons salt
¼ teaspoon cinnamon
dash of cayenne
2 tomatoes, peeled, seeded, and chopped
2 cups fresh green beans, cut into 1½-inch pieces, or 2 cups
*   fresh or frozen peas*
2 tablespoons tamari or soy sauce

☐ Soak the garbanzo beans for at least 4 hours (overnight is best). Discard soaking water.
☐ After they have soaked, cook them in 6 cups of water over medium heat for 1½ hours, or until they are tender.
☐ In a soup pot, sauté onions in olive oil until soft. Add garlic, celery, and sweet potato (or squash or carrots). Sauté another 5 minutes.
☐ Add stock and all herbs and spices except tamari. Bring to a boil, then reduce heat to a simmer (cover pot). Simmer for 30 minutes. Add tomato, green beans, and cooked garbanzo beans. Simmer, uncovered, until vegetables are tender, approximately 10 to 15 more minutes.
☐ Add tamari. Taste and adjust seasoning. Serve with plain or garlic croutons. Serves 8 to 10.

White Bean and Squash

This is a surprisingly light and elegant bean soup. We like this soup's subtle bean flavor, and it is a good first course for any meal.

> 1 cup dried navy beans
> 5 cups water
> 1 tablespoon olive oil
> 4 cloves garlic, chopped
> 1 large shallot, chopped
> 1 medium onion, chopped
> 3½ cups peeled and cubed (1-inch) winter squash (see
>   instructions on page 175)
> ½ teaspoon dried basil
> ½ teaspoon dried oregano
> ¼ teaspoon dried thyme
> 4 cups Vegetable Stock (see recipe on page 44)
> salt and pepper to taste
> ¾ cup half and half or soy milk (optional)

☐ Wash beans and cover with 5 cups water in a large pot. Bring to a boil, reduce heat, and simmer, covered, for approximately 1½ hours or until beans are tender. Drain.
☐ In a soup pot, sauté garlic, shallot, and onion in 1 tablespoon olive oil for approximately 5 minutes.
☐ Add cubed squash, cooked beans, herbs, and stock. Bring to a boil, then reduce the heat, and simmer, covered, until squash is tender, approximately 20 minutes.
☐ Purée soup in batches in blender.
☐ Return to soup pot, add half and half or soy milk, and taste to adjust seasoning. Add salt and pepper to taste. Serves 6.

Golden Potage

This assortment of sweet root vegetables produces a very soothing soup. No single vegetable dominates, resulting in a delicate flavor. We like to make this in the fall and early winter, when root vegetables are freshest and at their sweetest.

3 tablespoons vegetable oil
1 cup chopped leek or sweet onion
8 cloves garlic, chopped
1 to 1½ cups diced sweet potato or winter squash
½ cup chopped parsnip
½ cup chopped carrot
1½ cups diced potatoes
4 cups Vegetable Stock (see recipe on page 44)
1 teaspoon salt
½ cup half and half or soy milk
1 tablespoon chopped fresh herbs, such as thyme or marjoram
    (or 1 teaspoon dried herbs)

☐ Sauté leek or onion and garlic in oil for 5 to 8 minutes. Add the rest of the vegetables and sauté for 10 more minutes.

☐ Combine sautéed vegetables and soup stock in a large soup pot. Add salt. Bring to a boil, and then reduce heat to a simmer. Simmer, covered, for 30 minutes.

☐ Cool slightly, and purée in 2 batches until creamy. Return soup to the pot and add cream and herbs. Taste, adjust seasoning as needed. Serves 6.

Wild Rice and Mushroom

Wild rice soup is a favorite among people who visit and live in Minnesota, and harvesting wild rice in the fall has been a Minnesota tradition for many generations of native Ojibwa Indians. This soup is well suited for festive holiday meals.

> ¾ cup wild rice
> 7 cups Vegetable Stock (see recipe on page 44)
> ⅓ cup long grain brown rice
> rosemary—dried or fresh, a generous sprinkling
> 2 tablespoons olive oil
> 1 medium onion, chopped
> 2 large carrots, diced
> 2 stalks celery, diced
> 3 tablespoons butter or olive oil
> 1 pound mushrooms, sliced
> 2 cups half and half
> ¼ cup parsley, chopped
> 1 cup white wine (optional)
> salt and pepper to taste

☐ Wash wild rice thoroughly.

☐ Bring stock to a boil, add wild rice, brown rice, and rosemary. Simmer, covered, for 1 hour or until rice is tender. While rice is cooking, chop vegetables.

☐ Sauté onion, carrot, and celery in olive oil for about 10 minutes. When rice is tender, add vegetables to the rice.

☐ Take 2 cups of the vegetable-rice mixture and purée in blender; add purée to soup.

☐ Sauté mushrooms in butter or oil. Purée half of the sautéed mushrooms with the half and half, and add to soup.

☐ Add the rest of sautéed mushrooms, parsley, wine, salt, and pepper. Simmer soup, uncovered, until heated through, but do not let it boil. Serves 6 to 8.

BREADS

YEASTED BREADS

QUICK BREADS

Yeasted Breads

At the Cafe, we offer a basket of organic breads with dinner. Included are a whole wheat sourdough and corn bread. During the holidays, we often add a variety of festive breads, many of which are included here. Bread often makes a meal out of a bowl of soup and always adds a homey touch to any meal. Baking bread is very satisfying, too: Nothing can compare to the aroma and flavor of fresh-baked bread.

Yeast-raised breads take time, but are easy to make. We have a basic recipe for Whole Wheat Bread, but we're presenting you with many variations so you can create a new loaf every time you bake bread. When you are comfortable with the recipe, you will come up with your own variations as well. If you are unsure of the process or have any doubts, refer to either the whole wheat recipe or to the following discussion of techniques.

Yeast: We use active dry yeast in all of our recipes. It is readily available and dissolves well. Yeast is killed by high temperatures (above 140°) and is limited in its growth by low temperatures (below 80°). We recommend a temperature of about 100° to 110° F. for dissolving the yeast. You need not measure your water's temperature, because if the water is over 110° it will feel very hot. Use water that is comfortably warm to the touch.

Kneading: Kneading is essential to good bread. Turn the dough onto a lightly floured surface, and knead with the hands by turning, pushing, and folding the dough for 5 to 10 minutes, or until it is smooth and elastic. Add small amounts of flour if the dough is sticky. Try not to add more flour than you need. Overkneading and too much flour result in a tough, dry loaf.

Raising: After you knead it, put the dough in a large, oiled bowl. Turn the dough over in the bowl to oil both sides. This keeps the dough from sticking to the bowl and forming a crust on the top. Cover the bowl with a towel, and place it aside to rise until doubled. Find a warm (80° to 85°) spot, away from drafts. I often use my oven, warming it slightly and turning it off before placing the bread inside. To check whether the dough is ready, insert 2 fingers into it. If the dough has not risen enough, the depression will fill quickly; if the finger holes remain, the dough has risen enough.

Pans: We always butter our loaf pans, because oil tends to be absorbed, which causes sticking. Butter the pans or baking sheets well. A standard loaf pan is 9 inches long, 5 inches wide, and 3 inches deep. This is the size we use in our recipes, although any variance will result in only a size difference.

Baking: Always preheat your oven before baking bread. If your oven has hot spots or it is fairly full, check the loaves for uneven browning and rotate the pans to even out the heat. To test whether bread is done, tap the bottom of a loaf. If it has a hard, hollow sound, the bread is done. If the loaf is soft and sounds dense, return it to the oven for an additional 5 to 10 minutes, and then test it again.

Freezing: To preserve freshly baked bread, freeze it. First cool loaves to room temperature. Put each loaf into a plastic bag, or wrap each loaf tightly in plastic.

Thaw bread at room temperature. Reheat a thawed loaf in a 350° oven for 15 minutes. You may also thaw a frozen loaf in the oven. Preheat the oven to 325°, and allow 30 to 40 minutes for the bread to warm.

Whole Wheat and Variations

This is a basic bread recipe. It produces a rich, brown loaf with a slight honey taste. You may increase the amount of honey for a sweeter loaf. Following this recipe are several variations that include different grains, sesame seeds, dried fruit, or nuts. Experiment with the recipe, and you will find a new taste every time you make bread!

2 cups warm water
2 tablespoons active dry yeast
½ to ¾ cup honey
¼ cup vegetable oil
1 tablespoon salt
5 cups whole wheat flour
2 to 3 cups unbleached white flour

☐ Dissolve yeast in warm water. The water should feel slightly hotter than body temperature (about 100° to 110°), but it should not be so hot that it kills the yeast. Add honey, oil, and salt. Stir well. Add both whole wheat and unbleached white flour 1 cup at a time, stirring well after each addition.

☐ When dough is stiff and forms a rough ball, turn it onto a floured surface. If dough is manageable before you have added all the unbleached white flour, turn it out and knead in as much flour as you need until dough is not sticky. Knead dough for 5 to 8 minutes, repeating a rhythmic push, turn, and fold. Dough should be soft and elastic, springing slightly when pinched.

☐ Oil a bowl. Put dough in the bowl, turning to coat all sides with oil. Cover and let rise in a warm place. Let rise until doubled, about 1 hour.

☐ Punch down and knead several times to work out the air bubbles. Reshape the dough into a ball and put it back into the bowl. Cover the bowl, and let the dough rise again until doubled, about 30 to 45 minutes. (Letting the dough rise a second time is not absolutely necessary, but it results in a finer textured loaf. We usually let the dough rise twice when we use a lot of whole wheat flour.)

☐ Punch the dough down and shape it into 2 loaves. Place each loaf in a buttered loaf pan. (Always prepare pans with butter, margarine, or vegetable shortening instead of oil. Dough does not rise easily in an oiled pan, and the oil is often absorbed by the dough, causing the loaf to stick.) Cover loaves with a cloth, and let them rise again for 20 to 30 minutes, until doubled.

☐ Bake the loaves in an oven preheated to 350° for 45 minutes to 1 hour. To check a loaf, tap on the bottom crust. If the loaf sounds hollow and hard, it is done. If the loaf feels soft and sounds dense, return it to the oven and check it again in 5 to 10 minutes. Cool the loaves on a rack completely before slicing. Store in a plastic bag. Makes 2 loaves.

VARIATIONS

Bran: Follow the above recipe, but substitute molasses for the honey (or use part honey and part molasses). Add 1½ cups bran when you add the whole wheat flour, and use only 2 cups of whole wheat flour. Add up to 4 or 4½ cups unbleached white flour. You may want to add ½ cup raisins.

Corn-rye: Follow the above recipe, but substitute the following flours for the whole wheat flour: 1 cup cornmeal, 2 cups rye flour, and 2 cups whole wheat flour. Add unbleached white flour as needed.

Nut: Follow the above recipe, but add 1 cup finely chopped nuts before you add the flour. Try peanuts, pecans, or walnuts.

Millet: Bring 1½ cups water to a boil, and stir in ½ cup millet. Return to a boil, and then reduce to a simmer. Simmer, covered, for approximately 30 minutes or until all water is absorbed. Let cool. Follow the recipe for Whole Wheat Bread. Add the cooked millet to the dough before you add the flour. The millet loaf is good when it is made with half whole wheat flour and half unbleached white flour, approximately 7 to 8 cups total flour.

Oat: Follow the above recipe. Add 1 to 1½ cups rolled oats when you add the flour. The oat flavor tends to come through better if you use more unbleached white flour than whole wheat flour, so we like to use 2 cups of whole wheat flour and 5 to 5½ cups of unbleached white flour. Try brushing the top of the loaf with egg white and sprinkling with oats just before baking.

Sesame: Follow the above recipe. Add 1 cup of plain or lightly toasted sesame seeds when you add the flour. If you combine sesame seeds and rolled oats in the same loaf, you will get a moist loaf with a crunch. Use 1 cup toasted sesame seeds and ½ to ¾ cup rolled oats in all. As suggested under the oat variation, brush the loaf with egg white and sprinkle with toasted sesame seeds, rolled oats, and a little salt.

TOASTING SESAME SEEDS
To toast sesame seeds, dry-roast them in a small sauté pan on top of the stove over medium heat. Stir constantly for about 3 minutes or until they begin to pop and turn light brown.

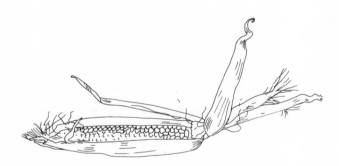

Cheddar Cheese

Cheese seems an unlikely ingredient in a yeasted bread recipe, but it makes a wonderful golden loaf with a soft and smooth texture, and it makes great toast! For a spicy, Southwestern touch, add chopped jalapeño peppers along with the Tabasco™.

> *2 cups warm water*
> *2 tablespoons active dry yeast*
> *4 tablespoons butter*
> *¼ cup honey*
> *1 tablespoon salt*
> *2 cups (6 ounces) finely grated sharp cheddar cheese*
> *½ to 1 teaspoon Tabasco™ sauce*
> *5 to 6 cups unbleached white flour*

☐ Dissolve yeast in warm water.

☐ Melt butter. Add butter and honey to yeast mixture. Stir to combine. Add salt, cheese, Tabasco™, and 2 cups flour. Beat until smooth. Continue adding flour, 1 cup at a time, until dough is stiff. Turn onto a floured surface.

☐ Knead dough for 10 minutes, adding more flour until dough is not sticky. Dough will be very soft and pliable. It should bounce back to shape when pressed with a finger. If it is over-kneaded or has too much flour, the dough will be hard. Put dough in a buttered bowl, turning to butter the top. Cover bowl, and let rise in a warm place until double in size, about 1½ hours.

☐ Punch down dough, divide in half, and shape into 2 loaves. Place in buttered loaf pans. Cover pans and let rise again until doubled, about 45 minutes to 1 hour.

☐ Bake loaves in a preheated 375° oven. Check oven after 20 minutes: If loaves are browning too quickly, cover them with aluminum foil. After a total of 35 minutes, check to see if bread is done by tapping on the bottom crust. If in doubt, check with a cake tester or a knife. Tester should come out clean and dry.

☐ Makes 2 loaves.

Cornmeal

Cornmeal gives this bread a fine texture and a rich, yellow color. When buying cornmeal, seek out a coarsely ground natural or organic meal. There is no comparison.

> ½ cup honey
> 4 tablespoons butter
> 1 cup scalded milk
> 1 cup boiling water
> 1½ cups yellow cornmeal
> ½ cup warm water
> 2 tablespoons active dry yeast
> 1 tablespoon salt
> 3 to 4 cups unbleached white flour (4½ to 5½ cups if using
>   all white flour)
> 1½ cups whole wheat flour (optional)

☐ Put honey and butter in a large bowl. Pour scalded milk and boiling water over the honey and butter. Stir until butter melts and combines with the honey. Slowly add the cornmeal, stirring to combine. Let stand until lukewarm.

☐ Dissolve the yeast in the warm water. Add the yeast mixture and salt to the cooled cornmeal mixture. Add flour 1 cup at a time, stirring well after each addition. If you are using whole wheat flour, add it first. Then add as much white flour as you need (about 3 cups) to get a dough that holds together and is not sticky. Turn the dough out onto a floured surface.

☐ Knead dough, adding more flour until dough is smooth and elastic. Total kneading time should be at least 5 minutes.

☐ Put dough in an oiled bowl. Cover and let rise in a warm place until doubled, approximately 1½ hours.

☐ Turn dough out of the bowl. Knead briefly to get out the air bubbles. Divide the dough in half and shape into 2 loaves. Place loaves into buttered loaf pans. Cover and let rise again until doubled, which should take approximately 45 minutes.

☐ Preheat oven to 350°. Bake for 45 to 50 minutes. Bread is done when it is golden brown and sounds hollow when tapped. If the bread sounds dense, return it to the oven and check it again in 5 minutes. Turn out of the pans to cool. Cool completely on a rack before slicing. Makes 2 loaves.

SCALDING MILK

To scald milk, heat the milk in a saucepan over direct heat or in the top of a double boiler over (not in) boiling water. Milk is scalded when tiny bubbles form around the edges of the pan. Remove from the heat before it comes to a boil.

Cinnamon

Cinnamon bread is a special treat as toast. This is a cinnamon dough rolled with cinnamon, honey, and nuts. It looks as good as it tastes. Try raisins or other dried fruit for added sweetness.

1½ cups scalded milk
½ cup honey
½ cup warm water
2 tablespoons active dry yeast
1 tablespoon salt
1¼ teaspoons cinnamon
¼ cup vegetable oil or melted butter
4 cups whole wheat flour
1½ to 2 cups unbleached white flour
¼ cup honey or maple syrup
½ cup chopped pecans or walnuts
½ cup raisins (optional)

☐ Scald the milk. Combine the hot milk and the honey in a large bowl. Let sit until lukewarm.
☐ Dissolve yeast in warm water. Stir into the cooled milk mixture. Add salt, 1 teaspoon of the cinnamon, and oil or melted butter. Stir until well mixed. Add flour 1 cup at a time. Stir well after each addition until dough holds together and is not very sticky.

☐ Turn out dough onto a floured surface. Knead for 5 to 10 minutes, adding more flour until dough is no longer sticky and springs back when pressed.

☐ Put dough in an oiled bowl. Cover with a towel and let rise in a warm place until doubled, approximately 1½ hours.

☐ Turn out dough onto a lightly floured surface and divide in half; set half aside. Roll the dough into a rectangle measuring 8 by 12 inches. Drizzle honey or maple syrup over the dough, using about 2 tablespoons. Sprinkle with cinnamon, ¼ cup nuts, and ¼ cup raisins on the dough. Roll up the dough, starting with the 8-inch side. Pinch the ends together and put in a buttered loaf pan. Repeat with the other half of the dough. Cover the pans with a towel. Let bread rise in a warm spot for about 1 hour.

☐ Bake in a preheated 350° oven for 50 to 60 minutes. The bread is done when the loaves have browned and sound hollow on the bottom. Turn out of the pans to cool. Let cool completely before slicing. Makes 2 loaves.

Hearty Wheat with Cracked Wheat and Wheat Germ

This recipe produces a dense loaf with a rough texture. It makes a nice sandwich bread. For a lighter loaf, use part white flour.

2 cups boiling water
¾ cup cracked wheat
½ cup honey
½ cup warm water
2 tablespoons active dry yeast
1 tablespoon salt
¼ cup vegetable oil or melted butter
½ cup wheat germ
4½ to 5 cups whole wheat flour

☐ Pour boiling water over cracked wheat and honey. Stir. Let sit until at room temperature.
☐ Dissolve yeast in warm water. Add yeast, salt, oil or melted butter, and wheat germ to cracked wheat and stir to combine. Add 2 cups flour to make a wet, spongy mixture. Let sit for 15 minutes.
☐ Add the rest of the flour, 1 cup at a time, stirring after each addition until dough is workable. Turn out onto a floured surface, and knead 3 to 5 minutes until dough is smooth and elastic.
☐ Put dough in an oiled bowl. Cover and let rise in a warm place until doubled, approximately 1 hour. Punch down dough and cover again, letting it rise a second time for 45 minutes to 1 hour.
☐ Divide dough into 2 equal pieces. Shape into loaves and put in 2 buttered loaf pans. Cover loaves and let rise a third time, until doubled, for about 30 minutes.
☐ Preheat oven to 350°. Bake loaves for 45 to 50 minutes.
☐ Turn loaves out of pans and tap on the bottom. Bread should sound hollow, not dense. If bread is not done, put loaf back into pan and bake a little longer. When bread is done, place on a rack to cool. Makes 2 loaves.

Savory Herb

This a favorite in the summer when fresh herbs are abundant, but it can also be made with dried herbs (cut the herb quantities in half). You can also make this recipe with whole wheat flour, but if you use all whole wheat, you will lose a lot of the herb flavor. Combine 2 cups or less whole wheat with enough white flour to satisfy the quantity.

1½ cups warm water
1½ tablespoons active dry yeast
¼ cup honey
4 to 4½ cups unbleached white flour
1 teaspoon chopped fresh summer savory
2 teaspoons chopped fresh chives
2 teaspoons chopped fresh parsley
1 teaspoon chopped fresh thyme
other herbs: marjoram, basil, or oregano (use a total of 2
tablespoons)
1½ teaspoons salt
2 tablespoons vegetable oil

☐ In a large bowl, dissolve yeast in warm water. Add honey and 2 cups of flour. Stir well. Let mixture sit while you chop the herbs. Add herbs, salt, and oil. Stir well.

☐ Add remaining flour 1 cup at a time. When dough is stiff, turn onto a floured surface and knead, adding flour until dough is not sticky. Dough should be soft and bounce back when lightly pinched.

☐ Put dough in an oiled bowl. Cover and let rise in a warm place for 1 hour.

☐ Turn out dough onto a floured surface. Knead a few times to get rid of air bubbles, and divide dough into 2 equal portions. Shape dough into round, slightly flattened loaves, and place them on opposite ends of a buttered cookie sheet. Herb Bread may also be shaped into loaves and baked in buttered loaf pans. Cover and let rise again for 45 minutes to 1 hour.

☐ Preheat oven to 350°. Bake for 50 minutes to 1 hour. Loaves will be browned with a hard crust that sounds hollow when tapped. Makes 2 loaves.

Maple-Pecan English Muffins

English muffins are a lot of fun to make and are a reasonable alternative to fresh bread during the summer. These muffins cook on top of the stove in a heavy skillet. This basic English muffin recipe uses maple syrup and pecans, but you can use honey in place of the maple syrup and try different nuts—or eliminate them altogether. The muffins will keep well for a few days and are a real treat for breakfast when made the night before.

½ cup warm water
1 tablespoon active dry yeast
½ cup boiling water
½ cup plain yogurt
3 tablespoons maple syrup
¾ cup ground, roasted pecans (see roasting instructions on
*   page 21)*
2 cups whole wheat flour
1 teaspoon salt
½ teaspoon baking soda
1 cup white flour
cornmeal for dusting muffins

☐ Dissolve yeast in warm water.

☐ Mix boiling water and yogurt together in a large bowl. Add dissolved yeast, maple syrup, ground nuts, and 1½ cups whole wheat flour. The dough will be loose and spongy. Cover and let rise in a warm place, until doubled in size, about 1 hour. You can let it sit longer, even overnight. It will rise and fall several times, getting increasingly sour as it sits.

☐ After the dough has doubled, sprinkle the salt and soda on top. Stir to combine. Stir in remaining ½ cup whole wheat flour. Add white flour in small amounts, stirring after each addition until dough is stiff and can be turned out onto a floured surface.

☐ Knead dough, adding as much flour as you need until you have a pliable, slightly sticky dough. Return dough to a clean, oiled bowl, cover, and let rise a second time. The second rising should take about 30 minutes.

☐ Punch down dough and turn onto a floured surface. Roll out with a rolling pin until it is ½ inch thick. Cut into 3- to 4-inch circles with a biscuit cutter or the rim of a glass. Dust both sides with cornmeal and set on cookie sheets to rise once more. This third rising takes 45 minutes to 1 hour. While rising, the muffins will take on their own shape. If you prefer perfectly round muffins, you may either purchase English muffin tins or make your own tins with saved tuna cans.

☐ Cook muffins 10 minutes per side on a griddle or in a heavy skillet, over medium-high heat. Yields 8 to 9 large muffins.

Oatmeal

This is a rich, moist bread that keeps well. For a less rich version, omit the milk and use 2 cups of water. Oatmeal Bread is a good way to use up leftover oatmeal: Simply replace all or part of the rolled oats with cooked oatmeal.

1 egg white
1 tablespoon water
2 cups rolled oats
⅓ cup honey
¼ cup butter or shortening, room temperature
1 cup boiling water
1 cup scalded milk
¼ cup warm water
2 tablespoons active dry yeast
1 tablespoon salt
2 eggs, slightly beaten
5 to 6 cups unbleached white flour or part whole wheat (up to
   3 cups) and part white flour

☐ To make the egg wash, mix 1 egg white with 1 tablespoon water, and set aside.
☐ Put oats, honey, and butter or shortening in a bowl. Pour in boiling water and scalded milk. Stir until butter melts. Let sit until lukewarm.
☐ Dissolve yeast in warm water. Add to cooled oat mixture. Sprinkle salt over the top and stir in. Add eggs and 2 cups flour. Mix well. Continue to add flour, 1 cup at a time, mixing well after each addition. When dough holds together and is not too sticky, turn onto a floured surface. Knead for 5 to 8 minutes, adding more flour as needed.
☐ Put dough in an oiled bowl and cover with a towel. Set in a warm place, and let rise until doubled, approximately 1 hour.

☐ Punch down dough and knead briefly to get the air out. Divide dough in half and shape into 2 loaves. Place in well-buttered loaf pans. Brush the tops of the loaves with egg wash and sprinkle the top with rolled oats. Set aside to double again. The second rising will take about 30 to 45 minutes.

☐ Bake in a preheated 350° oven for 45 to 50 minutes. To check loaves, turn them out of the pans and tap the bottoms. They should sound hollow. If they sound dense, let bake a little longer. Turn bread out of the pans, and let them cool on a rack. Makes 2 loaves.

Pumpernickel Rye

Pumpernickel Rye is a dark, moist bread with a very rich flavor. It is good with potato soup and sharp cheddar cheese.

1½ cups warm water
2 tablespoons active dry yeast
½ cup dark molasses
1 tablespoon salt
1 tablespoon caraway seed
2 tablespoons melted or very soft butter
¼ cup cocoa
2½ cups rye flour
2½ cups unbleached white flour
cornmeal

☐ Dissolve yeast in warm water. Stir in molasses, salt, caraway seed, butter, cocoa, and rye flour. Beat vigorously until smooth. Stir in unbleached white flour 1 cup at a time until dough is ready to handle.

☐ Turn dough onto a floured surface. Knead for about 5 minutes, adding more flour until dough is smooth and not sticky. Dough should feel soft and pliable, not hard.

☐ Put dough in an oiled bowl and cover with a towel. Place in a warm spot to rise until double, about 1 hour.

☐ Punch down dough and then round it up again. Cover and let rise again until double. The second rising takes approximately 40 minutes.

☐ Butter a baking sheet and sprinkle it with cornmeal.

☐ Punch down dough and divide it in half. Form into 2 round loaves and place on opposite corners of baking sheet, leaving room for them to rise again. Cover loaves and let them rise again until double, approximately 1 hour.

☐ Bake in a preheated 375° oven for 30 to 40 minutes. Bread is done when it sounds hollow on the bottom. If bread sounds dense, return it to the oven for a few more minutes. Cool before slicing. Makes 2 loaves.

VARIATION: ORANGE-GINGER PUMPERNICKEL

Here's an idea: Make a loaf of original Pumpernickel Rye and a loaf of Orange-Ginger Pumpernickel, or double the orange and ginger quantities to 4 tablespoons of each to make 2 Orange-Ginger loaves.

2 tablespoons orange peel
3-inch piece fresh ginger root

☐ Cut away the peel of an orange, avoiding the bitter white part. Slice peel very thin and chop coarsely.

☐ Peel the ginger. Slice thin and chop coarsely, making about 2 tablespoons.

☐ Follow the directions for the Pumpernickel Rye. Divide dough in half before adding the white flour. Add 2 tablespoons orange peel and 2 tablespoons ginger to half of the dough. Add white flour, and continue preparing each bowl separately (as directed in the original recipe).

Potato

Potato Bread is a great way to use up leftover mashed potatoes, but once you've made this bread, you'll go to the trouble of making mashed potatoes just for a couple of loaves. This is a light, flavorful loaf with a nice texture. It is wonderful toasted and also makes nice sandwich bread.

> 2 medium potatoes, peeled and boiled (enough for 1 cup
>   mashed potatoes)
> ¼ cup warm water
> 1½ tablespoons active dry yeast
> ⅓ cup butter, room temperature
> 2 tablespoons honey
> 1 tablespoon salt
> 1½ cups warm potato water
> 6 to 6½ cups unbleached white flour (or 3 cups whole wheat
>   and 3 cups unbleached white)

☐ Boil and mash potatoes, and set them aside to cool. Reserve 1½ cups water from cooking potatoes.

☐ Dissolve yeast in warm water.

☐ In a large bowl, combine butter, honey, and salt. Pour in potato water, stirring until butter melts. Whisk in mashed potatoes. Combine dissolved yeast with mashed potato mixture.

☐ Add flour 1 cup at a time until dough will hold together in a ball. Turn dough onto floured surface. Knead, adding more flour until dough is not sticky and feels soft and pliable.

☐ When dough is fully kneaded, put in an oiled bowl. Cover with a towel, and move the bowl to a warm place to rise. Raise 1½ hours until doubled. Punch down and knead for a minute or so to get out any air bubbles. Cut in half and shape into 2 loaves, and put them in buttered loaf pans. Cover pans and let sit until dough doubles, about 30 to 40 minutes.

☐ Bake in preheated 400° oven for 15 minutes. Reduce heat to 350° and bake for an additional 25 minutes. For crustier bread, remove the loaves from their pans and put them directly on oven shelves for 5 more minutes. Loaves will be golden brown and sound hollow when tapped. Makes 2 loaves.

Whole Wheat French

French bread dough is so easy to make—it is amazing that something so good can come of so few basic ingredients. This recipe has no shortening in it, so it is best eaten the same day it is made. If you cannot eat it that day, freeze it. To freeze, wait until bread is cool, and then wrap it very tightly in plastic or place it in a plastic bag.

> *1½ cups warm water*
> *1½ tablespoons active dry yeast*
> *2 cups unbleached white flour*

☐ Dissolve yeast in the warm water. Add the flour, and stir until well-mixed. It will be a very loose sponge. Let it sit in a warm place covered well for 2 to 8 hours. We often make the sponge at night and let it rise overnight, finishing the bread in the morning. The mixture will rise and fall several times if left overnight or all day. The longer it is left, the better the flavor it will have.

> *2 teaspoons salt*
> *½ cup warm water*
> *3 cups whole wheat flour*
> *½ to 1 cup unbleached white flour as needed*

☐ Dissolve salt in the water. Stir salt water into the sponge. Add flour, 1 cup at a time, until you have a workable dough. Turn dough onto a floured surface, and knead for 10 minutes. The dough will be smooth and elastic.

☐ Put the dough in an oiled bowl. Turn it in the bowl to oil both sides. Cover with a towel and let dough rise in a warm place.

☐ When dough has doubled (about 1½ hours), turn the dough out onto a floured surface and knead lightly for a minute to press out any air. Divide the dough into 3 pieces and shape into baguettes or rounds. Place on buttered baking sheets, leaving plenty of space between them. Cover the loaves with a towel, and put them in a warm place to rise until doubled. This takes 45 minutes.

☐ Preheat the oven to 375°. To get the crisp crust, try to create a moist oven: Several minutes before the bread goes in the oven to bake, place a large, low pan on the lower shelf. Pour about 1 cup of boiling water in the pan. Let the oven fill up with steam. Then bake the loaves on the middle shelf. The water will evaporate in the first 15 minutes.

☐ Bake the loaves for approximately 45 minutes. Bread is done when it is golden brown and sounds hollow on the bottom. Remove from the oven and cool on a rack. Makes three 14-inch baguettes.

CREAM

We try to cut back on high fat creams such as heavy or whipping cream, which contains 36 to 40 percent milk fat. We use soy milk as often as possible, and suggest it as a substitute for cream in sauces and soups. Soy milk is rich in protein and low in fat and carbohydrates and has no cholesterol. When we feel a recipe will be enhanced by a little richness, we add half and half, which contains 10½ to 18 percent milk fat, reserving the use of heavy cream for special occasion desserts.

Festive Fruit

We usually associate yeasted fruit breads with the holidays, but here is a loaf that is welcome all year long. Serve it for breakfast or as dessert.

¾ cup scalded milk
6 tablespoons butter, cut into small pieces
⅓ cup honey
½ teaspoon salt
¼ cup warm water
1 tablespoon active dry yeast
1 egg, slightly beaten
½ teaspoon nutmeg
3½ to 4 cups flour
1 cup chopped cranberries
½ cup raisins
¾ cup chopped walnuts
1 cup chopped dates
1 tablespoon grated orange rind

☐ Combine scalded milk with butter. Stir to soften butter, and then add honey and salt. Cool to lukewarm.

☐ Dissolve yeast in ¼ cup warm water. Add yeast and egg to milk and stir to combine. Add nutmeg and 2 cups flour. Let sit while chopping fruit and nuts.

☐ Add cranberries, raisins, nuts, dates, and orange rind. Stir well. Continue adding flour, approximately 1½ cups, until dough is stiff enough to turn out and knead.

☐ Turn out onto a floured surface and knead, adding small amounts of flour until dough is not sticky. Knead about 5 minutes. Put in an oiled bowl and cover. Let rise in warm place until doubled, about 2 hours.

☐ Punch down and shape into 2 round, slightly flattened loaves. Place on opposite ends of a buttered cookie sheet. Cover and let rise again for 45 minutes to 1 hour or until doubled.

☐ Bake in a preheated 350° oven for 40 to 45 minutes. Bread is done when loaves sound hollow, not dense, when bottom is tapped. Place on a rack to cool.

☐ Festive Fruit Bread may be baked in 2 large or 3 small loaves. Two loaves measure about 8 inches across the top, and 3 loaves measure 5 to 6 inches across the top.

Cardamom

The smell of freshly ground cardamom is truly wonderful. If you can't find fresh cardamom, you can substitute the preground spice, but nothing compares to the flavor and aroma of grinding the seeds right before they are used. We grind ours with a mortar and pestle.

We think of this as a festive loaf, filled with spices, orange zest, and nuts. Serve it on a special occasion or during the holiday season.

¼ cup warm water
2 tablespoons active dry yeast
½ cup scalded milk
¼ cup butter
½ cup honey
¼ cup orange juice
1 teaspoon salt
18 cardamom pods, shelled and ground (or ½ teaspoon ground seeds)
¼ teaspoon cinnamon
4½ to 5 cups unbleached white flour
2 eggs, slightly beaten
½ tablespoon orange zest
egg white
sliced or slivered almonds

☐ Combine yeast and warm water in a small bowl, and set aside.
☐ Scald milk and add butter. Stir to melt butter, and then add honey, orange juice, and salt. Stir to combine and set aside to cool. When mixture is lukewarm, add ground cardamom, cinnamon, and 2 cups of flour. Beat until smooth. Add eggs, yeast, and orange zest.
☐ Add remaining flour 1 cup at a time until dough is a slightly sticky mass. Turn onto a floured surface. Knead, adding flour until dough is not sticky. Knead a minute or 2 more. Put in an oiled bowl, cover, and let rise in a warm place until dough doubles, about 2 hours.

☐ Punch down dough and divide in half. Shape each half into a round, slightly flat loaf and place on opposite ends of a buttered cookie sheet. Let rise until doubled, about 1 hour.

☐ Brush top with beaten egg white and sprinkle with almonds. Bake in a preheated 350° oven for 30 to 45 minutes. Bread will be golden brown and sound hollow when the bottom is tapped. Makes 2 round loaves.

☐ Cardamom Bread is festive when baked in a braid! After the dough has risen for the second time, divide each half into 3 equal portions. Roll the thirds into ropes. Pinch 3 rope ends together, and loosely braid the dough. Pinch the opposite ends to keep the braid together. Let the braided loaves raise until doubled, about 1 hour, on a well-buttered cookie sheet. Bake as directed. Makes 2 braided loaves.

Apricot

When you want some delicious baking fruit in the middle of the winter but the choices are few, there are always dried apricots! This is a sweet, spicy loaf that goes well with afternoon tea or Sunday brunch. You can use some whole wheat pastry flour in place of the white for a heartier texture.

½ cup boiling water
1 cup chopped dried apricots
2 tablespoons butter
½ cup honey
1 egg, slightly beaten
1 cup plain yogurt
½ cup rolled oats
2 cups unbleached white flour
1 tablespoon baking powder
½ teaspoon baking soda
½ teaspoon salt
¼ teaspoon nutmeg
¼ teaspoon ground ginger
½ cup chopped pecans
2 teaspoons grated orange rind (optional)

☐ Pour ½ cup boiling water over chopped apricots and let it sit while you prepare bread dough.
☐ In a large bowl, cream butter. Add honey and beat until well blended. Add egg and yogurt. Mix well.
☐ In a separate bowl, combine oats, flour, baking powder, baking soda, salt, and spices. Stir into butter mixture. Drain apricots well and fold in with nuts and orange rind.
☐ Pour into a buttered loaf pan. Bake in a preheated 350° oven for 45 to 50 minutes. Bread is done when a cake tester inserted in the middle comes out clean. Let cool for 10 to 15 minutes, and then turn out onto a rack and cool completely before slicing. Makes 1 loaf.

Banana-Wheat

We grew up on banana bread. It still is a favorite snack for kids. This hearty recipe is not too heavy and is very tasty.

1 cup butter, room temperature
⅔ cup honey
4 eggs, slightly beaten
2 tablespoons plain yogurt
2 teaspoons lemon juice
2 teaspoons vanilla
6 very ripe bananas, mashed
1 teaspoon baking soda
1 tablespoon baking powder
½ teaspoon salt
3 cups whole wheat flour or part whole wheat and part
*   unbleached white flour*
1 cup wheat germ
1 teaspoon cinnamon
1 cup chopped walnuts or pecans
1 cup chopped dates (optional)

☐ Cream butter. Add honey and beat until smooth. Add eggs and beat until combined. Add yogurt, lemon juice, vanilla, and bananas. Stir to combine.

☐ Combine dry ingredients in a separate bowl. Add to wet ingredients, and stir until well mixed. Add nuts and dates if desired. Pour into 2 buttered loaf pans.

☐ Bake in a preheated 350° oven for 60 to 70 minutes. Test with a cake tester. It should come out clean. Let loaves cool in the pans for 10 to 15 minutes. Then turn out onto a rack and let cool completely before slicing. Makes 2 loaves.

Blueberry-Lemon

You can make this loaf with either fresh or frozen berries, but we have had better luck with fresh ones. Frozen berries bleed easily and tend to sink to the bottom of the loaf.

To prevent the fruit from sticking to the bottom of the pan, put the loaves into the oven right after you turn the batter into the pan. A honey-lemon glaze makes a nice sweet and tart topping.

½ cup butter
¾ cup honey
2 eggs, lightly beaten
½ cup plain yogurt
1 teaspoon salt
1 tablespoon baking powder
3 cups unbleached white flour
grated rind of 1 lemon
1 cup blueberries
juice of 1 lemon
honey to taste

☐ Cream butter. Add honey and beat until well blended. Add eggs and yogurt, and beat again until blended.

☐ In a separate bowl, combine dry ingredients. Stir into wet ingredients until just blended. Fold in lemon rind and blueberries. Pour into a buttered loaf pan.

☐ Bake in a 350° oven for 50 to 60 minutes. Check loaf with a cake tester. Bread is done when cake tester comes out clean.

☐ Remove bread from oven and cool in the pans for 10 minutes, then turn them out onto a wire rack. While the bread is still warm, cover it with a thin glaze made with the juice of a lemon sweetened with honey. Wait until bread is completely cooled before slicing. Makes 1 loaf.

Buttermilk Scones

Scones are quick and easy morning biscuits. They are the best when handled the least: Stir until just mixed, and then knead as little as possible. We use dates in this recipe, but any dried fruit will work. Try adding some nuts or spices, too: The possibilities are endless! One of our favorites is listed at the end as a variation.

¾ cup unbleached white flour
1 cup whole wheat pastry flour
½ teaspoon baking soda
½ teaspoon cream of tartar
½ teaspoon salt
½ cup well-chopped dates
½ cup buttermilk
1 egg, room temperature, slightly beaten
2 tablespoons melted butter, cooled

☐ Preheat oven to 450°.
☐ Combine dry ingredients. Mix well. Stir in the dates.
☐ In another bowl combine buttermilk, egg, and melted butter. Stir well. Gradually stir into flour mixture.
☐ Turn out onto a floured surface. If it seems too sticky add a little flour. Knead briefly, only once or twice.
☐ Divide dough into 4 pieces. Pat each piece into a 5-inch circle. Cut each circle in half.
☐ Bake on a buttered cookie sheet for 10 to 15 minutes. Scones are done when lightly browned. If you're unsure, test with a cake tester. It should come out clean. Scones are best eaten warm. Makes 8 scones, but this recipe is easily doubled.

VARIATION: BUCKWHEAT SCONES

Use 1¼ cups white flour and ½ cup buckwheat flour. These are good when dried apricots replace the dates.

Classic Pecan Coffee Cake

This is a classic coffee cake recipe with a cinnamon-nut-sugar mixture sprinkled through the layers. Combining the baking soda and yogurt and allowing it to rest gives the soda more leavening power, which creates a rich, moist cake. This recipe can also be made in a 9 x 13-inch cake pan—try swirling the nut mixture through the top with a knife.

1½ cups plain yogurt or sour cream
2 teaspoons baking soda
1 cup coarsely chopped pecans
2 teaspoons cinnamon
3 tablespoons date sugar (available at natural food stores)
3 cups unbleached white flour
2 teaspoons baking powder
1½ teaspoons salt
4 tablespoons butter, room temperature
1 cup honey
3 eggs
1 tablespoon vanilla

☐ Blend yogurt or sour cream with baking soda. Cover and let stand at room temperature for ½ hour.

☐ Mix chopped pecans with cinnamon and date sugar. Set aside.

☐ Combine flour, baking powder, and salt.

☐ Beat butter until smooth. Add honey and beat until well blended. Add eggs, vanilla, and yogurt or sour cream mixture. Beat well. Add dry ingredients and stir until just combined. Do not overbeat.

☐ Butter a 12-cup Bundt pan. Cover bottom of pan with a thin layer of batter. Sprinkle half of the nut mixture over batter. Add another thin layer of batter and the rest of the nuts. Pour the remaining batter into pan. Smooth the top with a spoon or spatula.

☐ Bake in a preheated 350° oven until cake tests done, approximately 45 minutes. Let cool for 5 to 10 minutes in the pan. Invert onto a wire rack, and remove pan. Let cool before slicing.

Coconut-Orange

This tropical-tasting bread makes us think we're in a faraway land with the ocean at our feet! The coconut creates a moist, chewy loaf that is delicious and exotic tasting.

3 tablespoons butter
½ cup honey
2 eggs
1 teaspoon vanilla
¼ cup fresh orange juice
2 cups flour
1 tablespoon baking powder
¼ teaspoon salt
½ cup unsweetened coconut
1 tablespoon grated orange rind (optional)

☐ Cream butter. Beat in honey until smooth and creamy. Add eggs and beat until incorporated. Add vanilla and orange juice.
☐ In a separate bowl, combine dry ingredients. Stir into wet ingredients. Fold in coconut and orange rind. Pour into a buttered loaf pan.
☐ Bake in a preheated 350° oven for 45 to 50 minutes. Bread is done when a cake tester inserted in the center comes out clean. Let loaf cool for 10 to 15 minutes, then turn out onto a rack. Cool completely on the rack before slicing. Yields 1 loaf.

Cranberry

Along with wild rice, cranberries are a popular food in Minnesota. Here is our version of the traditional cranberry sweet bread. It is as pretty as it is delicious.

¼ cup butter, room temperature
½ cup honey
1 cup orange juice
1 egg, slightly beaten
2 tablespoons grated orange rind
2 cups whole wheat flour
2 teaspoons baking powder
½ teaspoon baking soda
½ teaspoon salt
½ cup chopped nuts—walnuts or pecans
1 cup cranberries, coarsely chopped

☐ Cream butter. Add honey and beat until light and creamy. Add orange juice, egg, and orange rind, beating until well mixed.

☐ In a separate bowl, combine dry ingredients. Stir into wet ingredients just until combined. Stir in nuts and cranberries.

☐ Turn dough into buttered loaf pan. Bake in a preheated 350° oven for 50 minutes to 1 hour. Bread will be done when a cake tester inserted in the middle comes out clean. Let bread stand in pan for 10 to 15 minutes, and then turn out onto a cooling rack. Cool completely before slicing. Makes 1 loaf.

Pumpkin

This bread is equally good when sweet potato or winter squash is substituted for the pumpkin.

> 1 cup mashed, cooked pumpkin (canned or fresh)
> ⅓ cup butter
> ½ cup honey
> 2 eggs
> 1 cup whole wheat flour
> 1 cup unbleached white flour
> ½ teaspoon baking powder
> 1 teaspoon baking soda
> ½ teaspoon salt
> 1 teaspoon cinnamon
> ½ teaspoon ground ginger
> ½ cup chopped nuts
> ½ cup raisins (optional)

☐ To cook fresh pumpkin, clean, peel (see instructions on page 175), and cut the pumpkin into 2-inch chunks and steam it for 15 to 20 minutes until soft. (Or to bake, halve the pumpkin, clean out the seeds, and place on a baking dish with a little water. Bake at 350° for 40 to 50 minutes or until soft.) Mash the pumpkin to get 1 cup.

☐ Beat butter, add the honey, and beat until creamy. Add eggs and pumpkin. Beat again until well-combined.

☐ Combine dry ingredients in a separate bowl. Gradually stir into pumpkin mixture. Stir in nuts and raisins.

☐ Spoon mixture into a buttered loaf pan. Bake in preheated 350° oven for 50 minutes to 1 hour. Bread is done when a cake tester inserted in the center comes out clean. Let the loaf cool for 10 to 15 minutes and then turn out onto a rack. Let cool completely before slicing. Makes 1 loaf.

Buttermilk Cornbread

This cornbread is rich and moist. Use ⅓ cup honey for a sweeter bread. Serve it with Black Bean–Vegetable Chili (page 154) or Stewed Pinto Beans (page 168).

> ½ cup butter or vegetable oil
> 5 medium eggs
> 2 cups buttermilk
> ¼ to ⅓ cup honey
> ¾ cup unbleached flour or whole wheat pastry flour
> 2½ teaspoons baking powder
> 1 teaspoon baking soda
> ½ teaspoon salt
> 2½ cups coarse-grind cornmeal (available at food coops and
>   natural food stores)

☐ Preheat oven to 350°.

☐ Melt butter. In a mixing bowl, beat eggs until light. Add buttermilk, honey, and melted butter.

☐ In a separate bowl, combine dry ingredients. Beat the dry ingredients into the wet mixture until smooth.

☐ Grease a 9 x 13-inch pan. Pour batter into pan and spread evenly. Bake for 30 to 35 minutes.

☐ Test with a cake tester or touch lightly in the center. The bread should spring back.

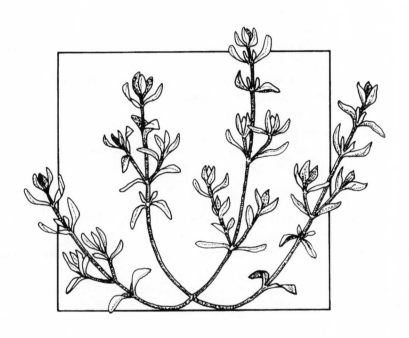

SEAFOOD & FISH ENTREES

Seafood and Fish

Few of us in the Midwest have good memories of the fish we ate while we were growing up, and we usually had fresh fish only when eating out. But, happily, good fresh fish has recently been available to many of us in our local markets.

Many people are unfamiliar with fish cooking methods, but really the worst thing you can do is overcook it. The more comfortable you are with the varieties of fish and fish cooking methods, the more you will cook with fish. Because fish and seafood are both very nutritious and easy to prepare, we hope our recipes entice you to cook with fish more often.

We have suggested specific fish to use with each recipe, but these are only guidelines. There are numerous other kinds of fish that you can substitute. Try to be flexible when planning a fish meal. Take advantage of what is available locally, because using what is freshest will always bring the best results. If you question what to substitute for a specific recipe, ask at the fish market or refer to a good fish and seafood cookbook that explains different fish families and their characteristics.

People are often unsure when a fish has finished cooking. There is a general rule that applies for all our cooking methods: Measure the fish at its thickest point, and calculate the cooking time at 10 minutes per inch. Fish is done cooking when its flesh is opaque. Because it continues to cook on its own after being removed from the heat, you can remove it when the center is barely translucent. Check this by inserting a sharp knife into the middle of one of the fillets.

Timing is the most important factor in preparing a meal with fish or seafood. The fish should always be the last item prepared, so try to ready the rest of the meal ahead of time and devote your attention to the fish.

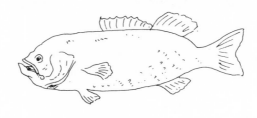

Broiled Mackerel with Orange-Miso Glaze

This is the same glaze used in the eggplant appetizer. You can prepare the glaze well ahead of time, and it will keep in the refrigerator for up to 2 weeks. The glaze, with its tangy ginger-orange combination, is a perfect match for rich mackerel. Only rice and a crunchy vegetable stir-fry are needed to complete a meal.

> *2 tablespoons orange juice concentrate*
> *1 tablespoon ginger juice*
> *2 tablespoons mirin*
> *3 tablespoons white or light miso*
> *1½ pounds mackerel fillets*
> *toasted sesame oil*

☐ Mix together the first 4 ingredients until smooth.

☐ Clean and dry the fish fillets, leaving the skin on. Lightly rub the bottoms of the fillets with toasted sesame oil, and place them in a baking dish.

☐ Spoon a generous amount of glaze on each fillet, and broil until the fish is opaque. Watch carefully: This will take approximately 10 minutes with the fish 3 to 4 inches from the flame. You can brown the glaze, but do not allow it to burn. Other fish suggestions: sole, halibut, mahimahi. Serves 4.

FRESH GINGER JUICE

Grate peeled fresh ginger very finely. Place the grated ginger in your hand and squeeze it over a bowl to extract the juice. Approximately 1 tablespoon of juice will come from a 2-inch piece of ginger.

You can freeze fresh ginger: Leave its peel on and wrap it well in plastic. The quality is not that of fresh ginger, but it is better than powdered ginger, which is not a good substitute for fresh ginger.

Poached Rainbow Trout or Salmon with Fresh Berry Vinaigrette

This is a very fresh, light way to sauce trout or salmon. We like to serve it with blanched asparagus or green beans and either boiled new potatoes or a simple rice pilaf with pecans. It is an extremely pretty and colorful plate and may be served hot or cold.

FRESH BERRY VINAIGRETTE

2 cups apple-blackberry juice
1 cup blackberries or raspberries (fresh or frozen)
juice of 1 lemon
½ cup walnut or canola oil
salt and white pepper to taste
whole berries for garnish

☐ Pour apple-blackberry juice into a saucepan, place over medium-high heat, and simmer until juice is reduced to ½ cup, approximately 10 minutes.

☐ Wash berries well. Purée them in a blender, and strain through a fine mesh strainer, removing seeds from the purée.

☐ Combine berry purée, juice reduction, and lemon juice in a bowl. Whisk in the oil, then seasonings, mixing until combined.

POACHED TROUT OR SALMON

4 cups water
1 onion, sliced
1 carrot, peeled and sliced
1 stalk celery, sliced
1 stem fresh parsley
3 to 4 whole star anise
3 bay leaves
½ teaspoon thyme
salt to taste
1 cup dry white wine
a few peppercorns
four 8- to 10-ounce trout or coho salmon

☐ Combine all of the above ingredients, except peppercorns and fish, in a saucepan. Simmer, covered, for 20 minutes. Throw in peppercorns and simmer for 5 more minutes. Strain and reserve stock.

☐ Pour strained stock into a shallow pan. Place fish in the pan with stock, and bring liquid to a simmer. Cover the pan if the fish are not immersed in stock. Gently simmer for approximately 6 to 8 minutes, depending on the thickness of the fish.

☐ Remove fish from pan as soon as they are done. Top with the vinaigrette, with additional berries as a garnish. Serves 4.

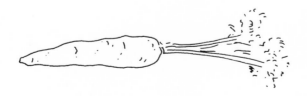

Caribbean Fish and Shrimp Stew

This is a wonderful fish stew with a rich and unique flavor. Coconut Milk is used as part of the stock, lending its richness. We have given directions on how to make your own Coconut Milk, but you can find canned coconut milk in Asian markets.

Make this stew with either shrimp or fish. If you are lucky enough to have some fresh conch, try it! It really is delicious. A loaf of bread or some flour tortillas with the stew makes a satisfying meal.

COCONUT MILK

1 whole coconut
3 cups water

☐ Place 1 coconut in an oven that has been preheated to 300°. The coconut will crack as the liquid and meat expand. It should take approximately 30 minutes.

☐ Open the coconut, reserving what liquid is left. Remove the meat from the shell: It should separate very easily. Cut the meat into ½-inch pieces.

☐ Boil 3 cups of water. Place 1½ cups of the water in a blender. Turn blender on high, and remove the center of the blender top.

☐ Add half of the coconut pieces 1 or 2 pieces at a time while the blender is running. When all of the first half of the pieces have been blended, pour the coconut-water through several thicknesses of cheesecloth or into a kitchen towel that you have placed in a strainer over a bowl. Squeeze the pulverized coconut in the cloth to extract the milk. Discard the coconut meat.

☐ Pour another 1½ cups of boiling water into the blender, and repeat with the other coconut half.

☐ A whole coconut yields about 3 cups milk.

SEAFOOD & FISH ENTREES

FISH STOCK

---

2 tablespoons butter or vegetable oil
1 onion or the green tops of a leek, chopped
4 cloves garlic, minced
fish scraps or shrimp heads and peels, reserved from cleaning
1 carrot, sliced
1 rib celery, sliced
1 tomato, diced (optional)
6 cups water (if using homemade Coconut Milk in stew, use
    only 5 cups water)

☐ Melt the butter in a soup pot. Sauté the onion or leek tops, garlic, and fish scraps for 3 to 5 minutes. Add carrot, celery, and tomato. Continue to sauté for another 5 minutes.
☐ Add water. Bring to a near-boil (don't allow it to boil), and then reduce heat, and gently simmer for 30 minutes. Strain, reserving liquid.

CARIBBEAN FISH AND SHRIMP STEW

---

1 tablespoon butter or vegetable oil
1 large onion, chopped
5 cloves garlic, minced
4 carrots, sliced
2 large potatoes, peeled and cut into 1-inch cubes
1 jalapeño pepper (optional)
2 ripe plantains or 1 yam, sliced thin
1⅓ cups canned or 3 cups homemade Coconut Milk
Fish Stock
1 pound shrimp
1 pound firm white fish, cut into 1-inch pieces
juice of 1 lime
salt and fresh ground black pepper to taste
sprigs of fresh cilantro for garnish

☐ Melt butter in a large soup pot. Sauté onion and garlic for 3 to 5 minutes, until onions are translucent. Add carrots, potato, and jalapeño, and sauté for 5 minutes. If using the yam, add the slices now.

☐ Add Coconut Milk and Fish Stock and bring to a boil. Reduce heat to a simmer, and cook, covered, until carrots and potato are quite tender, approximately 5 minutes.

☐ If you are using plantains, add them to the stew, and simmer for 10 minutes.

☐ Add fish and cook until flaky and tender, approximately 3 minutes. Turn off heat, add shrimp and stir, and then cover pot to allow shrimp to cook. Shrimp will turn pink when done. Add lime juice, and salt and pepper.

☐ Garnish each bowl with fresh cilantro. Serves 4.

Salmon with Cranberry-Mint Beurre Blanc

The unique, tart flavor of the cranberry balances the richness of the salmon beautifully. The sauce can be made low in fat: Simply leave out the butter and sweeten it up a bit with a little honey. Wild rice or potato purée and a green vegetable are nice accompaniments.

1 cup dry white wine
1 cup cleaned cranberries (fresh or frozen)
juice of 1 orange
6 tablespoons cold butter
½ teaspoon grated orange peel
½ tablespoon chopped fresh mint
pinch of salt
pinch of white pepper
1 tablespoon honey (optional)
4 to 6 salmon fillets (5 to 7 ounces each)
mint sprig for garnish

☐ In a saucepan bring wine, cranberries, and orange juice to a boil, and reduce the liquid down at a medium-high heat for 5 minutes.

☐ Blend cranberries and wine in blender until smooth.

☐ Pour cranberry purée into a saucepan and heat. Swirl cold butter into the purée, 1 tablespoon at a time. Add orange peel, chopped mint, salt, and pepper. If the cranberry purée is too tart, add a tablespoon of honey.

☐ Preheat broiler for 10 minutes. The high oven temperature will help seal in the juices.

☐ Place fillets on broiler rack, and position the rack so fillets are 2 to 4 inches from the heat. Fillets do not need turning. Check them after 5 minutes; they should be nearly done.

☐ Pour sauce over fish, garnish with mint, and serve at once. Serves 4 to 6.

Braised Tuna with Chinese-Style Vegetables

This is a complete meal. If you wish to serve more, we suggest a salad course. In the summer, we serve the rice noodles cold.

   You can substitute marlin or any other firm fish for the tuna. And, you can use other, more delicate seafood by changing the cooking process: Simply poach, steam, or broil the delicate fish separately.

1 to 1¼ pound fresh tuna, trimmed
½ cup cornstarch or arrowroot
1 heaping cup julienned carrots
1 heaping cup red sweet pepper, cut into strips
1 heaping cup sliced onions
1 heaping cup deveined pea pods
½ cup peeled and thinly sliced ginger root
1 small bulb garlic, minced
1 jalapeño pepper, minced (or ⅛ teaspoon cayenne pepper)
⅔ cup mirin
½ cup tamari or soy sauce
4 tablespoons rice vinegar
½ pound rice stick noodles
2 tablespoons vegetable oil
2 tablespoons sesame oil
ginger pickles (available from Asian grocery stores), sliced
     green onions, and fresh cilantro for garnish

☐ Cut trimmed tuna meat into ¼-inch thick strips. They should be no longer than 3 inches long and about 1 inch wide.
☐ Put the cornstarch or arrowroot and tuna in a brown paper bag, and shake it to lightly coat the tuna. Shake off excess cornstarch when you remove the tuna from the bag.
☐ Prepare all the vegetables.
☐ Combine mirin, tamari or soy sauce, and vinegar in a bowl. Stir well.

☐ Have a pot of boiling water ready for the rice noodles. They take about 5 minutes, depending on type of noodle (follow package instructions). The tuna cooks in only 6 minutes, so be sure to start the noodles just after you start the tuna.

☐ In a large sauté pan or wok, heat the vegetable and sesame oil. Lay strips of tuna in hot oil, and sauté briefly over high heat for about 1 minute. Turn them over, and immediately put in the garlic and ginger. Stir gently for approximately 1 minute, so the garlic gets sautéed briefly.

☐ Add the carrots, onion, and peppers.

☐ Pour in the mirin, tamari, and vinegar mixture, stir gently, and cover. Bring to a boil, turn down a bit, and simmer, covered, for a few minutes until vegetables are slightly crisp.

☐ Top the fish with vegetables and their sauce. If you prepare the fish without cornstarch, you may choose to thicken the bean sauce with a little cornstarch dissolved in water added to the sauce at the last minute.

☐ Be sure not to overcook the tuna. This all goes very quickly. At the last second add the pea pods.

☐ Serve immediately along with rice noodles. Garnish with ginger pickles, sliced green onions, and fresh cilantro. Serves 4.

RICE VINEGAR
Rice vinegar is a slightly sweet vinegar made from fermented rice.

Cod Fish Cakes with Horseradish–Sour Cream Sauce, Fresh Curry Mayonnaise, or Apricot Chutney

There are many, many ways to make fish cakes. This recipe works very well. You can play around with the seasonings, using what is in season or whatever you have on hand. Horseradish–Sour Cream Sauce is just one of the many sauces that go well with fish cakes, or try them with Fresh Curry Mayonnaise or Apricot Chutney. If fresh hake is available, it is just as good, if not better, for this recipe.

HORSERADISH–SOUR CREAM SAUCE

¾ cup sour cream or yogurt
1½ teaspoons Dijon mustard
2 tablespoons lemon juice
3 tablespoons freshly grated horseradish (or 1 tablespoon
prepared horseradish)
½ teaspoon salt
2 tablespoons chopped fresh dill (optional)
¼ cup milk

☐ Combine all the ingredients and mix well.

FRESH CURRY MAYONNAISE

1 egg yolk
1 tablespoon fresh lime juice
1 cup refined safflower oil
½ teaspoon salt
½ teaspoon curry powder
1 tablespoon ginger juice (see instructions on page 113)
pinch of cayenne (optional)

☐ In a mixing bowl, whip the egg yolk and lime juice together.
☐ Slowly add the oil in a light stream, beating constantly until the mixture begins to thicken. Continue beating the mayonnaise until all the oil is incorporated.
☐ Add salt, curry, ginger, and cayenne. Chill.
☐ Note: You can also make this with good prepared mayonnaise. Add the salt, curry, ginger, and cayenne to 1 cup prepared mayonnaise.

APRICOT CHUTNEY

1 cup dried apricots
½ cup golden raisins or currants
⅓ cup red wine vinegar
2½ cups water
¼ teaspoon cayenne (optional)
1 teaspoon fennel seeds
1½ tablespoons ginger root, finely grated
5 cloves garlic, minced
2 apples or pears, peeled and diced
pinch of salt

☐ In a saucepan, bring all ingredients to a boil. Reduce heat and cover pan. Simmer 45 to 60 minutes, or until chutney becomes glazed.
☐ Check occasionally to see if you need to add liquid. If you do, add water or apple juice.

COD FISH CAKES

1½ pounds fresh cod, cleaned and deboned
1¼ cups mashed, cooked potatoes
2 eggs, beaten
2 teaspoons salt
1 teaspoon fresh pepper
1 bunch green onion, minced
¼ teaspoon ground cardamom
1½ teaspoons grated orange peel
1 tablespoon chopped fresh cilantro
2 tablespoons chopped fresh parsley
flour or cornmeal for rolling cakes
4 tablespoons vegetable oil

☐ Grind up the cleaned cod in a food processor or grinder.
☐ Cook and mash potatoes. Set aside and cool.
☐ In a bowl, mix all remaining ingredients except vegetable oil together. Add cod and potatoes to mixture, shape into 2-inch patties, and roll the patties in flour or cornmeal.
☐ Heat vegetable oil in a sauté pan until hot. Sauté cakes until they are golden brown on both sides. They should be firm, but do not overcook. About 3 minutes on each side is plenty.
☐ Serve with Horseradish–Sour Cream Sauce, Fresh Curry Mayonnaise, or Apricot Chutney. It is also nice to serve these with more than one sauce. Makes 12 cakes.

Walleye Sautéed in Almond Meal

Many customers demand a phone call when we serve Walleye Sauteed in Almond Meal. We like to create a summer feast and serve it with sweet corn, potato salad, sliced tomatoes, and lemon wedges. The breading adds to both the flavor and the size of the serving, making a 4-ounce portion plenty for each person.

1 cup ground almonds
rind of 1 lemon, finely grated
½ teaspoon salt
¼ teaspoon cayenne pepper
¼ teaspoon black pepper
flour for rolling fillets
1 egg, beaten
1½ pounds walleye fillets
2 tablespoons butter, preferably clarified
2 tablespoons vegetable oil

☐ Combine almonds, lemon rind, salt, and cayenne and black pepper in a shallow bowl. First roll fillets in the flour, then dip them in the beaten egg, followed by the almond meal, turning to coat both sides well for all 3 coatings.

☐ Heat butter and oil until very hot in a large skillet. Reduce heat, and sauté fillets at medium heat until fillets are crispy and brown. This will take approximately 4 minutes for each side.

☐ Serves 4 to 6.

CLARIFYING BUTTER

Clarified butter is butter that has had the milk solids removed, leaving a butter that can be cooked at a higher temperature without burning as well as one that stores unrefrigerated for a longer time. Place unsalted butter cut into 1-inch pieces in a heavy saucepan over low heat. When the butter is melted, remove the pan from the heat and skim the froth from the top. Let the butter stand for a few minutes, allowing the milk solids to settle to the bottom. Strain the butter through a sieve lined with a double layer of cheesecloth. Pour the clarified butter into a jar, and store it, covered, in the refrigerator. Clarified butter loses about a fourth of its original volume.

North African Stuffed Trout with Tahini Sauce

This dish is excellent served with a salad of fresh orange slices, radishes, and red onion. Sprinkle the salad with lemon juice and olive oil. Steamed cauliflower or green beans are nice complements to the salad, as is French bread or couscous pilaf. And, of course, remember to serve olives!

STUFFING

---

4 tablespoons olive oil
4 cloves garlic, minced
½ cup minced shallots or onion
⅔ cup bread crumbs
1 tablespoon lemon juice
1 to 2 tablespoons chopped fresh cilantro or parsley
½ teaspoon salt

☐ Sauté the garlic and shallots or onions in 4 tablespoons olive oil for a few minutes.
☐ In a bowl, mix together the sautéed shallots and garlic with the rest of the ingredients. Salt to taste. Set aside.

TAHINI SAUCE

½ cup tahini
¼ cup plus 1 tablespoon buttermilk or yogurt
½ teaspoon dried coriander
3 tablespoons lemon juice, or to taste
3 tablespoons orange juice
cold water if needed
1 to 2 teaspoons chopped fresh mint
2 pinches of cayenne
½ teaspoon salt

☐ Whisk all of the sauce ingredients together until they are very smooth and creamy. Since tahini brands differ, you may need to add water to acquire a nice sauce consistency. If the tahini is lumpy, you may want to use a blender or food processor.

☐ Set aside and chill for approximately 15 minutes. After chilling, the sauce will most likely thicken. Add more water if you need to thin the sauce.

NORTH AFRICAN STUFFED TROUT

3 tablespoons oil or clarified butter
4 cleaned rainbow trout
flour for rolling fish

☐ Clean the trout and pat dry. Roll in flour.

☐ Divide the stuffing into 4 equal portions. Fill each stomach cavity of the trout with the stuffing.

☐ Carefully sauté the trout in a large sauté pan over medium heat in butter or oil until golden brown. This will take approximately 5 to 6 minutes on each side, depending on size of trout.

☐ Serve immediately with tahini sauce. Serves 4.

Sautéed Skate with Mango Relish

Skate is a true delicacy; it's richness and texture are reminiscent of crab. Skate is not always available, but this recipe works well with many varieties of fish that have been sautéed in clarified butter or olive oil.

MANGO RELISH

1½ cups peeled, seeded, and chopped mango
pinch of nutmeg
pinch of ground cloves
¼ teaspoon ground coriander
¼ teaspoon ground cardamom
2 to 3 tablespoons lime juice
½ tablespoon ginger juice (see instructions on page 113)
1 tablespoon chopped fresh mint
1 jalapeño, minced
pinch of salt
cayenne or chili paste to taste (optional)

☐ Measure out ¾ cup of the chopped mangos and set aside. Purée remaining ¾ cup of mangos until very smooth. Put the puréed mangos through a sieve and remove all the fibers.
☐ In a bowl, mix together the puréed and chopped mango. Add the nutmeg, cloves, coriander, cardamom, and lime juice.
☐ Add the ginger juice, chopped mint, and minced jalapeño to the mango mixture. Mix well. Season lightly with salt, and add cayenne or chili paste as desired. Serve either at room temperature or chilled. Makes enough relish for 6 medium-sized fillets.

SAUTEED SKATE

It's best to remove the meat from the cartilage of the skate wings. Ask at the market if they will cut the wings for you or show you how because it is different from filleting fish.

2 to 2½ pounds skinned and cleaned skate wings
vegetable or olive oil or clarified butter, enough for ⅛ inch in
bottom of pan
flour for dredging wings

☐ Dredge the skate wings in flour, and sauté in clarified butter or oil over medium-high heat. Cooking time varies depending on the thickness of the wings. Sauté on each side until flesh is opaque and lightly browned. Serves 6.

Japanese Broiled Scallops with Sautéed Spinach and Mustard Greens

Sea scallops have a wonderful rich quality, and so a light sauce like this one complements them well. The greens are a good, sharp contrast to the sweet scallops, and they go well together. You may use more spinach and less greens if you prefer a little less punch. Try Cucumber-Orange Salad (page 39) and Basmati Rice (page 141) as accompaniments.

JAPANESE BROILED SCALLOPS

¼ cup soy sauce
¼ cup cooking sake or mirin
½ to ¾ cup green onion, minced (1 bunch)
1½ pounds sea scallops

☐ Combine soy sauce, sake or mirin, and green onion to make marinade.
☐ Clean scallops: Pull off scallop muscle or foot, and rinse lightly in cold water.
☐ Place scallops in a 9 x 13-inch pan and cover with the marinade. Refrigerate and let sit for 30 to 60 minutes.
☐ Preheat broiler for 10 minutes. Broil scallops in the pan with the marinade for 6 to 8 minutes, being careful not to overcook the scallops. They are very tender and should be cooked only until they begin to turn opaque. Overcooking makes them rubbery. If you are using bay scallops, cut the cooking time approximately in half.
☐ As soon as you start broiling the scallops, start sautéing the mustard greens. Serves 4 to 5.

SAUTEED SPINACH AND MUSTARD GREENS

> 1 tablespoon toasted sesame oil
> 1½ tablespoons butter
> 4 to 5 large cloves garlic, chopped
> 1 bunch spinach, cleaned, destemmed, and slightly wet
> 1 bunch mustard greens, cleaned, destemmed, torn into
>   pieces, and slightly wet
> salt to taste

☐ In a hot skillet, melt sesame oil and butter together. Sauté the garlic until golden brown.
☐ Quickly add the wet spinach and mustard greens. Add salt, and cover the skillet. Check the greens after 1 minute: You may have to add a splash of water to help steam the greens and keep the garlic from browning. Cook for a couple of minutes altogether; greens will be wilted and soft.

Chinese Black Bean Sauce with Vegetable-Fish Stir-Fry

We like to serve this dish with rice noodles or rice, and it may be prepared with either fish or shrimp. Try serving rice noodles at room temperature in the summer.

If you have a large wok, you can stir-fry the fish and vegetables together. Or, cook the fish or shrimp separately, stir-fry the vegetables and sauce together, and serve the fish over noodles or rice, topping it with the sauce and vegetables at the last minute.

CHINESE BLACK BEAN SAUCE

> 3 cups water
> 1 medium onion, coarsely chopped
> 1 carrot, sliced
> 3 dried cayenne peppers (optional)
> 1 tablespoon star anise
> 1 teaspoon black peppercorns
> 1½-inch piece of fresh ginger root, thinly sliced
> 4 cloves garlic, smashed
> ½ teaspoon salt
> 1 large head of roasted garlic (see roasting instructions on
>   page 201)
> ⅓ cup mirin
> 2 tablespoons tamari or soy sauce
> ¼ cup rice vinegar
> ¼ cup Chinese fermented black beans (available at Asian
>   markets)

☐ In a saucepan bring water, onion, carrot, cayenne, star anise, peppercorns, ginger, smashed garlic, and salt to a boil. Turn heat down and simmer, covered, 20 minutes. Strain. Reserve the liquid and discard the rest.

☐ Combine mirin, tamari or soy sauce, rice vinegar, and black beans. Set aside to soak the beans while the stock is simmering.

☐ Roast 1 head of garlic in a 400° oven for approximately 20 minutes or until garlic feels soft.

Let it cool until you can handle it, and then squeeze out the garlic pulp from the skin, peeling the skin back a little if necessary.

☐ Whisk the garlic pulp into the stock. Add the black bean mixture. Set aside for later use in Vegetable-Fish Stir-Fry. Makes 3 cups.

VEGETABLE-FISH STIR-FRY

> 2 tablespoons toasted sesame oil (optional: Use only if
>   sautéing shrimp separately)
> 1¼ to 1½ pounds fresh fish or shrimp
> 2 tablespoons toasted sesame oil
> 1 small stalk broccoli, cut into florets
> 2 carrots, julienned
> 1 cup sliced enoki or shiitake mushrooms
> 1 red or yellow bell pepper, sliced
> 4 cloves garlic, chopped
> 1-inch piece of fresh ginger root, peeled and minced
> 1 bunch scallions, cut into 2-inch pieces (including green tops)
> 3 cups Chinese Black Bean Sauce
> 1 cup pea pods, deveined
> 2 tablespoons cornstarch or arrowroot dissolved in ½ cup
>   cooled Chinese Black Bean Sauce
> rice noodles (½ pound serves 4) or rice

☐ Fish: If you are using fish, clean and cut fish into large pieces—about 2 inches by 3 inches. Broil or sauté fish (while stir-frying vegetables) until just done. Place cooked fish on top of rice or noodles, and top with the sauce and vegetables, and serve.

☐ Shrimp: If you are sautéing the shrimp separately, heat 2 tablespoons toasted sesame oil in a sauté pan. Sauté the shrimp for a few minutes until just barely done and tender. Set aside, and cook the vegetables, adding the shrimp to the vegetables and sauce immediately before serving.

☐ In a large wok or sauté pan, heat 2 tablespoons toasted sesame oil. Add the broccoli and carrots and sauté for 2 minutes. Add mushrooms, bell peppers, and garlic, and sauté for 2 to 3 minutes.

☐ If you have enough room to stir-fry your fish with the vegetables, add it with the mushrooms and bell peppers.

☐ Add ginger, scallions, and sauce.

☐ Bring to a boil, and then reduce the heat and simmer for a few minutes.

☐ If you are using shrimp and you want to cook them with the vegetables, add them now.

☐ Add pea pods, and stir in the cornstarch that has been dissolved in sauce. Stir for a minute or two until it has thickened slightly.

☐ Serve on top of the rice or noodles (and fish or shrimp). Serves 4.

Sautéed Golden Tilefish with Kumquat-Shallot Glaze

Kumquat-Shallot Glaze is a light and delicate sauce that goes well with mild tilefish or sole. For a full meal, add a light grain such as couscous pilaf and perhaps sautéed greens or peapods.

> 1 tablespoon butter or vegetable oil
> ⅓ cup shallots, chopped
> 2 heaping tablespoons very thinly sliced kumquats
> ⅓ cup white wine
> ½ cup mirin
> juice from ½ lemon
> pinch of salt
> 1½ pounds tilefish fillets
> flour for dredging fish fillets
> 3 tablespoons butter or vegetable oil
> pomegranate seeds for garnish

☐ Heat butter or oil in a skillet. Sauté shallots for 3 minutes over medium heat. Add kumquats, wine, mirin, lemon juice, and salt. Cook over a high flame for a few minutes until it reaches a glazelike consistency.

☐ Dredge the fish fillets in flour, and sauté in 3 tablespoons butter or oil over medium-high heat.

☐ Serve glaze over sautéed fish, and garnish with pomegranate seeds. Serves 4.

Snapper Caribbean-Style with Ginger-Lime-Peanut Beurre Noisette served with Coconut Rice

Caribbean-style snapper with fried plantains and a rich, spicy sauce is a great way to serve fish for friends. Snapper is not always affordable, but rock fish is a good substitute. Make sure to find ripe plantains, which are yellow with dark brown spots and are soft to the touch. Serve this dish with Coconut Rice, sliced fresh mango, and sautéed greens for a Caribbean feast.

COCONUT RICE

☐ Cook rice according to package directions, but replace half of the water used for cooking the rice with Coconut Milk (recipe page 116). If desired, garnish the rice with toasted, shredded coconut.

SNAPPER CARIBBEAN-STYLE

---

2 tablespoons vegetable oil
2 to 3 ripe plantains
4 snapper fillets, 5 to 7 ounces each
3 tablespoons vegetable oil (if sautéing)
flour for dredging fish (if sautéing)
olive oil for brushing fish (if grilling)
4 to 6 tablespoons butter
1 to 2 jalapeños, minced
2 tablespoons lime juice
1½ tablespoons ginger juice (see instructions on page 113)
½ cup coarsely chopped, freshly roasted peanuts (see
    instructions on page 21)

☐ Peel the plantains. Sometimes the skin is difficult to remove, so try making 3 slits lengthwise from top to bottom, only as deep as the skin goes, making the skin easy to peel away.

☐ Slice the plantains diagonally into ¼-inch-thick slices. Sauté them over medium-high heat on each side in 2 tablespoons of vegetable oil until golden brown. Set aside.

☐ Sauté or grill fish. To sauté, dredge the fish in flour and sauté in 3 tablespoons vegetable oil until golden brown on each side. To grill, place fillets that have been brushed with olive oil directly on the grill, cooking for approximately 5 minutes on each side. Cook until fish is opaque. .

☐ While cooking the fish, prepare the sauce. It takes only a few minutes to assemble once you've prepared all the ingredients.

☐ In a very hot saucepan over a high heat, heat butter until it browns. Do not burn. Throw in jalapeños for 1 minute, and turn off heat.

☐ Add lime juice, ginger juice, and peanuts. Pour over fish and serve with plantains on the side. Serves 4.

Sautéed Halibut with Three Sauces: Harissa, Yogurt-Mint, and Tahini-Garlic

Often, we like to serve fish with more than one sauce. It is interesting and very flavorful, and these sauces can be quickly and easily prepared. The tahini and yogurt sauces can be made in advance and kept refrigerated until used. The Harissa, a North African red pepper sauce, is better prepared right before it is served. The sauce recipes below each make approximately 1 cup of sauce, enough for 8 medium-sized fillets.

We like to serve this with couscous, olives, and either green beans or sugar snap peas. We also suggest trying this with other white fish that is grilled, broiled, or sautéed.

HARISSA SAUCE
---

1 medium sweet red bell pepper, roasted (see instructions in Roasted Tomatillo Salsa and Cheese Quesadillas recipe on page 32) or sautéed until very soft (canned, roasted red bell peppers or sun-dried tomatoes can be used in place of the fresh pepper)
2 cloves garlic, peeled
⅛ to ¼ cup dried chilies
¼ teaspoon caraway seeds
¼ teaspoon salt
1 cup olive oil

☐ In a blender, purée together red pepper, garlic, chilies, caraway seeds, and salt.
☐ When mixture is smooth, add the olive oil in a slow, steady stream as blender is running.

YOGURT-MINT SAUCE

1 cup plain yogurt
1 teaspoon minced garlic
2 tablespoons lemon juice
1 tablespoon chopped fresh mint
salt to taste

☐ Combine all ingredients in a bowl and whisk together.

TAHINI-GARLIC SAUCE

⅓ cup tahini
2 tablespoons lemon juice
juice of 1 orange
1 teaspoon minced garlic
1 tablespoon chopped fresh parsley
salt to taste
⅓ cup water, or more as needed

☐ Combine all of the ingredients in a bowl. Whisk together until well combined. Add more water as needed to get a good sauce consistency. As the sauce sits it may thicken, so continue to add more water if needed.

SAUTEED HALIBUT

halibut fillets, 5 to 7 ounces each
flour for rolling fillets
vegetable or olive oil, enough for ⅛ inch in bottom of pan

☐ Clean and cut fish fillets into desired portions (usually 5 to 7 ounces each).
☐ Pat the fish dry, and roll each fillet in flour. Sauté the fish in vegetable or olive oil in a skillet over medium heat until done.
☐ Fish is done when the center of the thickest part of the fillet is opaque.

Baked Sole with Tarragon and Roasted Shallot–Garlic Butter

Fresh tarragon has a strong but subtle anise flavor, and it is easily grown in your garden. It is a great addition to many fish and vegetable dishes.

It can be difficult to find good fresh sole, so if it is unavailable, substitute any mild-tasting white fish such as mahimahi, snapper, or halibut. This is delicious served with a spinach and grapefruit salad and Basmati Rice.

BAKED SOLE

8 cloves garlic, roasted
2 shallots, roasted
1 tablespoon olive oil
1 large or 2 small leeks, white part only, julienned
½ cup dry white wine
3 tablespoons butter, room temperature
½ teaspoon salt
1 orange, peeled and cut into segments
½ tablespoon chopped fresh tarragon
½ tablespoon lemon juice
1½ pounds fresh sole, cleaned and trimmed

☐ Roast the garlic and shallots at 350° for about 20 minutes, until soft. Let cool briefly, and then peel shallots. Cut off the top of the garlic bulb with a sharp knife, hold on to the base of the bulb, and squeeze out the roasted garlic pulp.

☐ While the garlic and shallots are roasting, sauté leeks in 1 tablespoon olive oil for 2 minutes. Add wine and simmer, covered, for 3 to 5 minutes or until the wine has evaporated.

☐ In a blender or food processor, carefully combine the garlic pulp, shallots, butter, and salt. Set the garlic-shallot butter aside.

☐ Place the leeks in the bottom of a large, shallow casserole (at least 10 inches long) or 4 individual dishes.

☐ Put the orange segments, tarragon, and lemon juice into the casserole. Lay the sole fillets on top of this. Spread the garlic-shallot butter over the fish.

☐ Cover with lid or foil. Bake at 400° for 10 to 15 minutes. Depending on fillet thickness, the amount of baking time will vary. Watch carefully: It doesn't take long to overcook delicate sole.

☐ Remove from the heat when the center of the fillet is opaque. To check, insert a sharp knife into the thickest part of fillet and pull back gently. Serves 4.

BASMATI RICE

Basmati is a scented, long-grain rice. The literal translation of *basmati* is "queen of fragrance." Its aroma is often described as being similar to that of popcorn or as milky or nutty. Cooked basmati is slightly sticky, with long, slender grains. In India, there are dozens of varieties to choose from; you may find several here in Indian food stores, and food co-ops usually offer plain basmati or brown basmati.

To cook Basmati Rice: Wash 2 cups of rice. Place the rice in a saucepan with 2½ cups water and ½ teaspoon salt and cover. Bring the rice to a boil, and then turn the heat down and simmer, covered, approximately 15 minutes, until the water is all absorbed and rice is tender. Serves 4 (1 cup rice, cooked in 1½ cups water, serves 2).

Okisuki: Japanese Fish and Seafood Stew

This dish is often served right at the table and is usually made for no more than 4 people. Making the stew in larger quantities can make cooking and serving difficult.

When selecting a fish for the stew, choose one that will not fall apart easily. We suggest halibut, salmon, or snapper. We also recommend reserving some of the stock in which to poach the fish separately to assure that it does not get overcooked. This meal is very flavorful and warming—good for a fall or winter evening.

JAPANESE STOCK

6 cups water
two 3- to 5-inch pieces of kombu *seaweed*
1 cup bonito fish flakes
½ cup mirin
2 teaspoons salt

☐ Add *kombu* to water and bring to a boil. Add bonito flakes as soon as it comes to a boil. Immediately turn off the heat. Cover and let sit for 5 minutes. Strain. Add mirin and salt.

OKISUKI

1 pound fresh, firm fish (deboned and cut into 2-inch pieces)
¼ pound cleaned shrimp
1 3½-ounce package bean thread noodles
½ pound firm tofu, cut into 1-inch squares
½ cup mirin
1 sweet red or yellow bell pepper, sliced
1 cup mushrooms, quartered or halved (depending on the size)
2 bunches scallions, cut into 2-inch pieces
2 cups Chinese cabbage or greens
1 cup pea pods, deveined

☐ If you choose to cook the fish and shrimp separately, place ½ cup Stock in a sauté pan. Poach the fish in the stock as the vegetables are cooking. Watch the fish and shrimp carefully so that it does not overcook. Fish will take approximately 5 minutes; shrimp will cook in 2 to 3 minutes, depending on the size of the shrimp.

☐ In a shallow stock or soup pot, bring the stock to a boil. Add the bean thread noodles, tofu, mirin, bell pepper, and mushrooms.

☐ If you choose to cook the fish with the stew, add it with these vegetables. Bring this to a boil, and then reduce the heat. Simmer gently, covered, for 3 to 4 minutes.

☐ Add scallions and cabbage or greens, cover and simmer for 2 minutes. Add pea pods and let cook for a brief 30 seconds.

☐ Serve immediately. We find it easiest to bring the pot to the table. Ladle vegetables, tofu, and noodles into individual serving bowls, and top with fish or seafood. Serves 4.

SEA VEGETABLES (SEAWEED)

There are several types of sea vegetables farmed or harvested from the wild. Over 100 varieties are used worldwide. Most common to us are *hijiki, arame, nori, kombu, wakame,* and *dulse.* Sea vegetables are available at Asian food markets and food co-ops.

Sea vegetables are very good sources of minerals, proteins, and vitamins. They cleanse and purify our bodies, because they help to eliminate toxins. Studies also show that they reduce cholesterol.

We like to use sea vegetables in soups, salads, *nori* rolls, rice, and tofu croquettes as well as in condiments or side dishes.

Glazed, Sautéed Mahimahi with Sesame-Scallion Crust

At the Cafe, we make many different nut crusts for fish. This one is not only very tasty, but it is also very pretty. The whole, black sesame seeds combined with the ground seeds make an interesting speckled coating. You can also try this with rockfish, sea bass, or amberjack.

GLAZE

1 tablespoon soy sauce
2 tablespoons mirin or sake
2 tablespoons barley malt
1 tablespoon ginger juice (see instructions on page 113)
1 tablespoon lemon juice
2 tablespoons chopped scallions

☐ Combine all the glaze ingredients in a small bowl, and mix well.

SAUTEED MAHIMAHI WITH SESAME-SCALLION CRUST

¾ cup sesame seeds, white or brown
2 tablespoons black sesame seeds (optional, and available at
*   Asian food markets and food co-ops)*
2 to 3 tablespoons finely minced scallions
1 egg beaten with 1 tablespoon water
2 tablespoons vegetable oil
1½ to 2 pounds fish fillets

☐ Partially grind the white or brown sesame seeds in a food processor or food grinder. Combine the ground sesame seeds with the whole black sesame seeds and the minced scallions to make the sesame meal.
☐ Whip the egg and water together for an egg wash.
☐ Dip the fillets in the egg wash, and coat with sesame meal. Sauté in a skillet in 2 tablespoons hot oil until browned on both sides, and fish is done in the middle.
☐ Serve with the glaze spooned over the fillets. Serves 4.

Snapper Fillets with Cranberry-Ginger Sauce

Cranberries can usually be found during fall and winter. Get them when they are available, and freeze a bag for the summer months.

Cranberry-Ginger Sauce is good all year long. Ginger adds a spicy touch to the fruit glaze. New potatoes or a potato-parsnip purée and steamed snow peas go well with this dish.

CRANBERRY-GINGER SAUCE

1 cup cleaned, whole cranberries
1⅓ cups black cherry or other fruit juice
1 tablespoon orange rind
3 tablespoons mirin or sake sweetened with 2 to 3 teaspoons
*   of honey*
1 tablespoon ginger juice (see instructions on page 113)

☐ Combine cranberries, fruit juice, orange rind, and mirin or sake in a saucepan. Bring to a hard boil for 5 minutes to reduce the liquid.
☐ Remove from the heat and add ginger juice. Cool slightly, and purée in blender until very smooth. Set aside, keeping the sauce warm.

SNAPPER FILLETS

2 to 2½ pounds snapper fillets
flour for dredging fillets
2 tablespoons vegetable oil or clarified butter

☐ Cut snapper fillets into six 5- to 7-ounce portions.
☐ Dredge the fillets in flour, and sauté in a skillet with 2 tablespoons of hot vegetable oil or clarified butter.
☐ Serve with warm Cranberry-Ginger Sauce. Serves 6.

VEGETABLE ENTREES

North African Couscous-Vegetable Pilaf
with Harissa Sauce   180
Shepherd's Pie   182
Baked, Stuffed Squash with Leek-Orange Sauce   184

CROQUETTES

Buckwheat-Potato with Ginger-Mushroom Sauce   188
Chickpea-Vegetable with Tahini-Vegetable Sauce   190
Couscous-Almond with Orange-Shallot Sauce   192
Basmati Rice, Red Bean, & Vegetable with Salsa   194
Brown Rice, Almond, & Vegetable with
Roasted Onion–Miso Sauce   196
Roasted Eggplant Patties with Tomato-Basil Sauce   198
Butternut Squash, Cheese, & Walnut   200
Tofu, Vegetable, & Peanut with
Sweet & Sour Sauce   202
Wild Rice, Vegetable, & Pecan with
Wild Mushroom Cream Sauce   204
Tempeh-Potato with Spicy Peanut Sambal   206
Vegetable Pancakes   208

Carrot-Walnut-Cheese Loaf with Parsnip-Orange Sauce

Carrot-Walnut-Cheese Loaf is very popular at the restaurant, and can be just as popular at home. It can be prepared in advance and refrigerated until ready to bake; the ingredients are things we usually have in our kitchens; and the sauce is quick and simple but very rich in flavor and texture.

The loaf holds together well, but always let it cool down before you turn it out onto a platter. Serve with a crunchy vegetable salad and wild rice or a loaf of crusty French bread.

PARSNIP-ORANGE SAUCE

¼ cup butter or vegetable oil
2 parsnips
½ cup orange juice
½ cup white wine
1¼ cups water
pinch of salt

☐ Thinly slice the parsnips, and in a saucepan briefly sauté them in butter. Add the orange juice, wine, water, and salt.
☐ Simmer, covered, until the parsnips are tender, approximately 20 minutes.
☐ Transfer the mixture to a blender, and blend until smooth. The sauce may look a little thin but it will thicken when heated. Set aside.
☐ Return sauce to saucepan and heat gently before serving.

CARROT-WALNUT-CHEESE LOAF

2 tablespoons vegetable or olive oil
1 small onion, minced
2 cloves garlic, minced
4 to 5 large carrots, grated (approximately 4 cups)
½ pound mushrooms, coarsely chopped
¾ cup chopped, roasted walnuts (see roasting instructions on
  page 21)
1 cup bread crumbs
2 eggs
¼ cup half and half or soy milk
1½ cups grated Gouda or a nondairy soy cheese
½ teaspoon chopped fresh parsley
salt and pepper to taste

☐ Sauté onion and garlic in oil until soft. Add carrots and mushrooms and continue to sauté until tender, approximately 5 minutes.

☐ In a large bowl, combine the sautéed vegetables with the rest of the ingredients.

☐ Prepare a loaf pan by lining it with wax or parchment paper and then brush with oil. You may use the oiled pan without a lining, but a lined pan works better when you want to turn the loaf out to serve it.

☐ Spoon the mixture into the prepared pan. Cover with aluminum foil, and bake at 350° for 1 hour. Uncover loaf for the last 10 minutes and gently brown the top.

☐ Cool loaf in the pan for 10 minutes before turning out onto a platter. Serve with Parsnip-Orange Sauce. Serves 6.

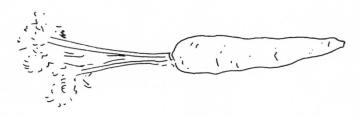

Black Bean–Vegetable Chili

At the Cafe, this has been a lunchtime favorite. We sprinkle our Black Bean–Vegetable Chili with grated cheese and Roasted Pumpkin Seeds. Serve the chili with Buttermilk Cornbread (page 107) or warm tortillas and salsa. This chili also makes a great filling for enchiladas!

2½ cups dried black beans
8 cups water for soaking
8 cups water for cooking
2 tablespoons olive or vegetable oil
1 large onion, chopped
4 cloves garlic, minced
2 large carrots, diced
2 stalks celery, chopped
1 sweet red bell pepper, seeded and chopped
2 to 3 jalapeño peppers, seeded and minced
1 tablespoon minced fresh marjoram (or 1 teaspoon dried marjoram)
1 tablespoon minced fresh oregano (or 1 teaspoon dried oregano)
1 tablespoon chili powder
1 tablespoon cumin
½ teaspoon cayenne
1½ teaspoons salt
½ teaspoon crushed coriander seed
juice of ½ lemon
1 ounce unsweetened chocolate

☐ Soak the black beans in 8 cups water for several hours or overnight.

☐ Drain the soaked beans, and cook them in 8 cups of water until tender (approximately 1 hour). Drain again, reserving cooking water.

☐ Sauté onion in olive or vegetable oil until soft. Add garlic, carrots, and celery. Continue to sauté for approximately 3 minutes, and then add red bell pepper and jalapeños. Sauté for an additional 3 to 5 minutes.

☐ Combine sautéed vegetables and cooked beans in a large pot. Add herbs and spices, lemon juice, and chocolate. Add 1 to 1½ cups bean-cooking water as needed.

☐ Simmer over low heat for at least 30 minutes. Serves 6 to 8.

ROASTED PUMPKIN SEEDS

Place the desired amount of pumpkin seeds in a sauté pan over a medium-high heat, and dry roast them on top of the stove for a few minutes, stirring constantly until seeds swell. Sprinkle a few drops of soy sauce over them, and cool the seeds.

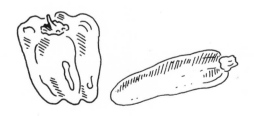

Burgundy Mushroom Stew

Burgundy Mushroom Stew is a savory dish that is good on a chilly day. Serve it with chunky garlic croutons or a loaf of Whole Wheat Oat (page 76) or Whole Wheat Millet bread (page 76). It's a nice, simple meal to serve to friends: Have them bring the salad!

   This recipe uses domestic button mushrooms, but a few wild mushrooms will add a great dimension to the stew. Simply sauté them along with the other mushrooms.

BROWN VEGETABLE STOCK

2 tablespoons butter or vegetable oil
1 parsnip, chopped
2 carrots, chopped
1 onion, chopped
2 cloves garlic, chopped
2 tomatoes, chopped
⅓ pound mushrooms, chopped
1 gallon water
celery leaves
leek tops (optional)
8 to 10 parsley stems
6 to 8 sprigs of thyme or 1 teaspoon dried thyme
20 peppercorns

☐ In a large soup pot, sauté vegetables in butter or oil until they quite brown and begin to stick. Cover with 1 gallon of water.

☐ Add celery leaves, leek tops, parsley, thyme, and peppercorns. Simmer briskly for 1 hour. Remove from heat and strain, reserving liquid.

BURGUNDY MUSHROOM STEW

3 tablespoons butter or vegetable oil
1 large onion, chopped
2 cloves garlic, minced
3 carrots, chopped
3 stalks celery, chopped
1 sweet red bell pepper, seeded and diced
4 cups Brown Vegetable Stock
1 cup red wine
3 large potatoes, peeled and cubed
2 teaspoons dried thyme
¼ teaspoon cayenne
¼ teaspoon dried marjoram
1 teaspoon salt
black pepper to taste
6 tablespoons butter or vegetable oil
6 tablespoons flour
3 tablespoons tomato paste
3 tablespoons butter or olive oil
1½ to 2 pounds mushrooms, quartered

☐ Sauté onion in 3 tablespoons butter or oil until soft. Add garlic, carrots, celery, and sweet bell pepper. Continue to sauté until vegetables are tender.

☐ In a large pot, combine Brown Vegetable Stock, wine, sautéed vegetables, potatoes, herbs, salt, and pepper. Cover and simmer over low heat while preparing the roux.

☐ To make the roux, melt 6 tablespoons butter or oil in a small saucepan. Add 6 tablespoons flour, mixing well. Cook the butter-flour mixture for 3 minutes, stirring to keep it from sticking.

☐ Whisk in 2 cups stew stock. Add tomato paste, and stir well. Pour roux into the stew. Stir to combine. Simmer, covered, until thick, approximately 5 minutes.

☐ Sauté mushrooms in 3 tablespoons butter or olive oil. Add to stew. Simmer until potatoes are done, approximately 10 to 15 minutes.

☐ Serve with garlic croutons. Serves 6 to 8.

Curried Chickpea and Vegetable Stew with Couscous

The curry spices in this dish make a fragrant and delicious stew. With the correct presentation, this is a very impressive meal to serve guests. Serve in bowls, with steamed green beans, black olives, and tomato wedges arranged on top of the stew. Garnish with fresh cilantro.

1 cup dried chickpeas
4 cups water for soaking
8 cups water for cooking
1 small eggplant
1 teaspoon salt
3 tablespoons olive or vegetable oil
1 medium onion, coarsely chopped
1½ tablespoons finely chopped garlic
2 medium potatoes, peeled and cut into ½-inch squares
½ medium buttercup or butternut squash or 1 large sweet potato, peeled and cut into 1-inch squares (see squash-peeling instructions on page 175)
2 tomatoes, chopped
¼ cup finely grated peeled ginger root
1 teaspoon turmeric
1 teaspoon chili paste (or 1 jalapeño pepper, chopped)
1 teaspoon ground coriander
1 teaspoon cumin seeds
1 teaspoon paprika
1 tablespoon curry powder
½ cup canned coconut milk (or 1 cup homemade Coconut Milk, recipe on page 116)
2 cups water or Vegetable Stock (see recipe on page 44)
½ tablespoon salt
½ head cauliflower, cut into florets
3 tablespoons lime juice
1 tablespoon tamari or soy sauce
2 cups couscous (see cooking instructions on page 180, and omit saffron when preparing couscous for this recipe)

☐ Soak chickpeas in 4 cups water for several hours or overnight.

☐ Drain the chickpeas. In a large pot, cover chickpeas with 8 cups of water. Bring to a boil, reduce the heat and let simmer, covered, until chickpeas are tender, approximately 1½ hours. Check occasionally to see if more water is needed. (To cook the chickpeas in a pressure cooker, cover beans in cooker with 6 cups of water. Bring to the correct pressure, and cook for 40 minutes.) Drain, reserving cooking liquid.

☐ Partially peel eggplant, leaving about half of the skin on. Slice lengthwise and cut into 1-inch pieces. Salt liberally, and set aside for 20 to 30 minutes, while the salt draws out bitter juices. Rinse the eggplant pieces thoroughly, and pat dry with a towel.

☐ Heat 2 tablespoons of the olive or vegetable oil, and sauté eggplant until golden brown, approximately 5 minutes. Set aside.

☐ In a pot large enough to accommodate the stew, heat the remaining 1 tablespoon of oil. Sauté the onion and garlic for about 2 minutes over medium heat. Be careful not to burn the garlic.

☐ Add the potato and squash or sweet potato. Sauté over medium-low heat for about 5 minutes. Add the tomatoes.

☐ Squeeze the grated ginger over the pan, squeezing the juice from the ginger into the stew. Add turmeric, chili paste or chopped jalapeño, coriander, cumin seed, paprika, and curry powder. Stir well, and cook for 1 minute.

☐ Add the cooked chickpeas, Coconut Milk, and stock or water. If more liquid is needed, add up to 2 cups chickpea cooking liquid or more stock. Add salt. Bring to a boil. Turn down the heat and simmer, covered, for 10 minutes.

☐ Add cauliflower, and simmer for another 10 minutes. Add eggplant, lime juice, and tamari or soy sauce. Stir a few times, and serve over couscous. Serves 4.

HOT PEPPERS

Hot or chili peppers differ in their degree of "heat." The compound capsaicin is the cause of the peppers' pungency, and is found in the seeds and the interior tissue of the pepper. It is wise to use caution when cooking with hot peppers. Wear thin rubber gloves for peeling and chopping the peppers, and beware of the possibility of the capsaicin being on your hands. Wash well before touching your face or eyes. If you feel a burning sensation, rinse with milk, which will help to neutralize the capsaicin.

Thai-Style Vegetable and Tofu Stew

This rich, tropical stew can be served year-round. Coconut combined with chili peppers and cilantro is a distinct flavorful blend. Serve with Basmati Rice (cooking instructions page 141).

THAI-STYLE STOCK

6 cups water
1 6-inch piece kombu *seaweed (optional)*
1 heaping tablespoon dried or fresh lemongrass root
2 hot chilies, dried
4 cloves garlic, crushed or minced
1 onion, sliced
1 carrot, peeled and sliced
1 teaspoon salt
4 bay leaves
½ tablespoon star anise
3 tomatoes, peeled and seeded
1 14-ounce can coconut milk (or 2½ cups homemade
*   Coconut Milk, recipe page 116)*
2 tablespoons barley malt (optional)

☐ Combine all ingredients except tomatoes, Coconut Milk, and barley malt in a saucepan.
☐ Bring the Stock to a boil, then turn down the heat and simmer, covered, for 20 minutes. Strain, reserving liquid in a medium-large soup pot.
☐ In a blender, combine the 3 tomatoes and Coconut Milk, and purée. Add this and the barley malt to the strained Stock.

STEW VEGETABLES

vegetable oil
½ pound tofu, cut into 1½-inch squares
1 heaping cup cubed potatoes
1 heaping cup 1-inch cubed squash or carrots
1 heaping cup 1-inch cubed cabbage
1 sweet red or yellow pepper, julienned
2 tomatoes, quartered
1 bunch scallions, cut into 1- to 2-inch pieces
2 tablespoons chopped fresh basil (or 2 teaspoons dried basil)
2 tablespoons fresh mint (optional)
1 tablespoon tamari or soy sauce
2 cups loosely packed fresh spinach, cleaned thoroughly and
*   destemmed*
1 heaping cup pea pods, deveined
lime juice to taste
½ cup coarsely chopped, roasted peanuts (see roasting
*   instructions on page 21) and chopped fresh cilantro for*
*   garnish*

☐ Lay cubed tofu on a well-oiled baking sheet. Turn to coat all sides with oil. Bake at 375° for 15 to 20 minutes.

☐ Bring the Stock in the soup pot to a boil. Add the cubed potatoes and the squash or carrots. Simmer, covered, for 10 minutes. Add the cabbage and sweet pepper and continue to simmer another 10 minutes.

☐ Add the baked tofu, tomatoes, scallions, basil, mint, and tamari or soy sauce. Re-cover and simmer 2 to 3 minutes.

☐ At the last minute, add the spinach and pea pods and cook them for 30 seconds to 1 minute. Add lime juice to taste.

☐ Serve immediately with Basmati Rice (cooking instructions page 141), using the roasted peanuts and fresh cilantro as garnish. Serves 4.

Greek Moussaka

Our version of this classic Greek dish uses lentils instead of the traditional lamb. It goes well with a Greek salad, Calamata olives, and pita bread.

TOMATO SAUCE

---

1 tablespoon olive oil

6 large cloves garlic, minced

2 cups peeled, seeded, and chopped tomatoes (you can use canned)

1 heaping tablespoon chopped fresh herbs: thyme, oregano, basil, mint, or sage (or 1 teaspoon dried herbs)

¼ teaspoon cinnamon

½ teaspoon salt

pepper to taste

½ cup pitted olives, chopped

☐ Briefly sauté garlic in olive oil: Do not brown it. Add tomatoes, herbs, seasonings, and olives. Simmer 5 to 10 minutes.

BECHAMEL SAUCE

1½ cups soy milk or milk

2 tablespoons vegetable oil or butter

2½ tablespoons unbleached flour

½ cup Parmesan cheese, grated (omit if making a non-dairy sauce)

salt and pepper to taste

pinch of nutmeg

☐ Using a small saucepan, bring milk to a boil, and then set aside.

☐ To make the roux, heat the vegetable oil or butter in another saucepan, add the flour, and stir for approximately 3 minutes until flour is slightly roasted. Add the hot milk, mixing quickly with a whisk.

☐ Add the Parmesan cheese and seasonings, continuing to whisk until well combined. Remove from the heat as soon as it thickens, before it comes to a boil.

GREEK MOUSSAKA

2 medium eggplants, enough to cover bottom of the casserole
    twice when sliced
2 teaspoons salt
olive oil for coating eggplant
1½ cups water, salted
½ cup lentils
2 cups ¼-inch-thick sliced potatoes
1 tablespoon olive oil
2 cups sliced onion
6 cloves garlic, minced
Tomato Sauce
Béchamel Sauce

☐ Partially peel the eggplant and slice lengthwise into ½-inch pieces. Liberally sprinkle the slices with salt and set aside for ½ hour while salt draws out any bitterness from eggplant. Rinse the eggplant and pat it dry with a towel.

☐ Rub the eggplant on both sides with olive oil. Lay them on a sheet pan, and broil the eggplant for 5 to 7 minutes on each side, or until golden brown. If you do not have a broiler, use a 450° oven and bake it for approximately 15 minutes.

☐ Cover lentils with 1½ cups salted water and bring to a boil. Reduce the heat and simmer for approximately 15 minutes, or until lentils are soft.

☐ Put sliced potatoes in a saucepan and cover with water. Bring to a boil, turn down, and simmer for approximately 5 minutes, or just until tender. Strain, and set aside.

☐ Sauté onion and garlic in 1 tablespoon olive oil over a medium flame for about 5 to 7 minutes. Onions should be very soft.

☐ In a 2½-quart casserole, layer the vegetables and sauces in the following order: potatoes, onion-garlic, lentils, Tomato Sauce, potatoes, eggplant, and Béchamel Sauce.

☐ Bake at 375°, covered, for 20 minutes. Remove cover and bake an additional 5 minutes. Serves 4 to 6.

Spinach, Zucchini, and Fresh Herb Gratin

Spinach, Zucchini, and Fresh Herb Gratin is quick to put together. Serve with couscous or rice and a medley of sautéed vegetables. For a lighter summer meal, serve with a loaf of French bread and a fresh fruit salad.

TOPPING

½ cup grated Parmesan cheese (optional)
½ cup bread crumbs
¼ cup pine nuts
1 tablespoon olive oil

☐ Mix the Parmesan cheese, bread crumbs, and pine nuts together with the olive oil. Set aside.

SPINACH, ZUCCHINI, AND FRESH HERB GRATIN

1½ pounds fresh spinach (approximately 2 cups cooked)
4 cloves garlic, minced
3 shallots, minced
1 small onion, minced
2 tablespoons olive oil
1 medium zucchini, diced
2 eggs
½ cup half and half or soy milk
1 teaspoon salt
½ teaspoon star anise powder
½ teaspoon grated orange rind
fresh cracked pepper
1 tablespoon chopped fresh herbs: basil, thyme, marjoram, or
    oregano (or ½ tablespoon dried herbs)
1 cup grated cheese: Swiss, Gruyère, or your favorite kind
    (optional)

164

☐ Wash spinach and pick off stems. Briefly steam the spinach until it is wilted. Set it aside in a colander to drain. Gently squeeze out excess liquid.

☐ Sauté garlic, shallots, and onion in 2 tablespoons olive oil over medium-low heat until onion is translucent. Add zucchini, and continue cooking until zucchini is lightly cooked, approximately 3 minutes.

☐ Combine all of the cooked vegetables in a food processor or blender. Add eggs, half and half or soy milk, salt, anise, orange rind, pepper, and herbs. Purée until just smooth.

☐ Pour the mixture into a bowl and add the grated cheese. Mix well.

☐ Pour spinach mixture into a buttered 2½-quart casserole or individual gratin dishes and top with bread crumbs.

☐ Bake at 375° for 35 to 40 minutes (2½-quart dish) or approximately 20 minutes (individual dishes). Gratin is done when the center is firm to the touch.

☐ Serve with lemon wedges. Serves 4.

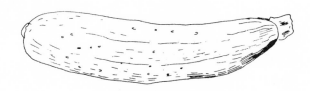

Vegetable Terrine Served on a Bed of Linguini

Vegetable Terrine takes a lot of time to prepare, but it is well worth the effort. It is as colorful and impressive as it is tasty. We like to serve it on a bed of linguini with a salad and Whole Wheat French Bread (page 93).

Allow 1 hour and 45 minutes for baking and cooling time. You may prepare vegetables in advance, but it is best to assemble the terrine right before baking it. If prepared vegetables have been refrigerated, bring them to room temperature before assembling, or it may take longer to bake.

8 teaspoons olive oil
2 sweet red bell peppers
1 large bunch spinach, cleaned thoroughly and destemmed
salt to taste
1 medium leek
1 medium parsnip
½ cup grated cheese (baby Swiss or Jarlsberg or soy
     mozzarella)
4 cloves garlic, minced
5 eggs
¾ cup half and half or soy milk
1 tablespoon tomato paste
2 teaspoons salt and pepper
1½ cups grated carrots

☐ Seed and thinly slice red bell peppers. Sauté lightly in 2 teaspoons olive oil; set aside.
☐ Measure out 6 cups of cleaned spinach by lightly packing in a large measuring cup. Briefly steam and then chop, salt lightly, and set aside in a colander to drain. Before assembling spinach in the terrine, squeeze spinach gently to extract as much water as possible.
☐ Clean the leek. Cut it in half and slice thinly. You should have ¾ cup. Sauté lightly in 2 teaspoons olive oil. Set aside to cool.
☐ Peel and grate the parsnip. You should have ¾ cup. Sauté lightly in 2 teaspoons olive oil, stirring often to keep it from sticking to the pan. Set aside to cool.
☐ When leek and parsnip are cool, combine them with the grated cheese.

☐ Preheat oven to 375°.

☐ Sauté garlic in remaining 2 teaspoons olive oil.

☐ Combine eggs, half and half or soy milk, tomato paste, salt and pepper, and sautéed garlic in a blender. Blend until smooth.

☐ Butter a 9 x 5-inch loaf pan and line with wax or parchment paper. Generously brush the paper with butter or oil.

☐ Spread spinach in the bottom of the pan, and press evenly in place. Pour in just enough egg mixture to barely cover the spinach.

☐ Next, spread a layer of grated carrots and pour in just enough egg mixture to barely cover them.

☐ Then, spread a layer of the leek-parsnip-cheese mixture. Again, pour in just enough egg mixture to barely cover the layer.

☐ Finish with the red bell peppers. Drain any liquid that may remain from sautéing them. Pour the remaining egg mixture over the peppers.

☐ Cover the loaf pan with aluminum foil. Set the assembled terrine in a larger pan filled with hot water. It is best if the water reaches at least halfway up the outside of the loaf pan.

☐ Bake for 1 hour and 25 minutes. Remove the foil for the last 15 minutes.

☐ Remove from the oven and let sit for 20 minutes before unmolding. To turn out terrine, run a knife around the outside of the wax paper and invert pan onto a platter. Remove the pan and peel away the paper.

☐ Serve terrine on a bed of pasta or rice. Dress pasta well with olive oil, garlic, and salt and freshly ground pepper. Serves 6.

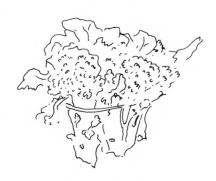

Sautéed Polenta with Stewed Pinto Beans or Fresh Tomato Sauce

This stewed pinto bean and polenta combination is a hearty and filling meal. A more elegant presentation for polenta is serving it with the Fresh Tomato Sauce and a Wild Mushroom Cream Sauce (page 204). Serve with a steamed green vegetable or summer squash.

STEWED PINTO BEANS

1 cup dried pinto beans
4 cups water for soaking
6 cups water for cooking
2 bell peppers, roasted (see instructions in the Roasted Tomatillo
    Salsa and Cheese Quesadillas recipe on page 32)
2 cups diced tomato
2 tablespoons olive oil
1 cup minced onion
8 cloves garlic, minced
1 tablespoon rosemary
½ teaspoon salt

☐ Prepare pinto beans ahead of time. Soak them for several hours in 4 cups water, and then drain, discarding soaking liquid. Cook the beans in 6 cups water for approximately 60 minutes or until soft. Drain, and discard liquid.

☐ Purée the roasted peppers in a blender with 1 cup of the tomato. Set aside.

☐ Sauté onions and garlic in 2 tablespoons oil in a skillet for 3 minutes. Add puréed pepper-tomato mixture, remaining diced tomato, pinto beans, rosemary, and salt. Simmer 10 minutes.

FRESH TOMATO SAUCE

1 tablespoon olive oil
1 tablespoon chopped garlic
3 to 4 cups peeled, seeded, and chopped fresh tomato (or
    canned plum tomatoes)

*1 to 2 tablespoons chopped fresh herbs (or ½ tablespoon
  dried)*
1 teaspoon salt
fresh ground pepper

☐ Heat olive oil in a medium saucepan. Add the garlic and sauté briefly.
☐ Add tomato and bring to a boil. Turn down the heat and simmer for 10 to 20 minutes. Add herbs, and season with salt and pepper.

SAUTEED POLENTA

Polenta can be heated in a skillet or on the grill. It is a nice accompaniment to grilled fish. Just lay polenta squares on a hot grill. Turn when polenta has been marked by the grill. If you turn it too soon, it will stick. Cook until second side is also marked and heated through.

5 cups water
½ tablespoon salt
*1¼ cups coarse-grind cornmeal (available at food co-ops and
  natural food stores)*
pepper to taste
3 tablespoons butter (optional)
olive or vegetable oil, enough for ⅛ inch in bottom of pan

☐ Bring water and salt to a boil in a medium-sized saucepan. Slowly add cornmeal, pouring it in a stream while stirring with a whisk to avoid lumps.
☐ Turn down the heat, and let it simmer over very low heat, stirring frequently, for 15 minutes.
☐ Stir in pepper, and butter.
☐ Pour into an oiled 9 x 9-inch pan. Refrigerate for 30 to 45 minutes or until firm.
☐ Cut polenta into 8 pieces. Sauté in very hot olive or vegetable oil. When the first side is golden brown, turn gently and sauté the second side until brown. The outside will be crispy, while the inside remains creamy.
☐ Serve the polenta with the Tomato Sauce spooned in ribbons over the squares and garnish with Parmesan cheese, or serve it with the Stewed Pinto Beans on the side garnished with sour cream and sprigs of parsley. Serves 4.

Eggplant, Roasted Walnut, and Asparagus Stir-Fry with Udon Noodles

We serve this stir-fry year-round, using asparagus in the spring and broccoli in the winter. Making the full-flavored broth ahead of time and refrigerating it makes this a quick meal to prepare. We often serve it with rice or rice noodles instead of udon noodles.

Udon noodles, a flat noodle made with wheat and occasionally rice flour, are available at natural food stores and Asian food markets.

BROTH
---

2 cups water
⅓ cup mirin
7 cloves garlic, chopped
2 tablespoons minced ginger root
1 carrot, peeled and sliced
2 bay leaves
¼ teaspoon ground anise (or a few whole star anise)
¼ teaspoon salt
1 to 2 chilies
1 teaspoon black peppercorns
2 tablespoons tamari or soy sauce
1 tablespoon barley malt (optional)

☐ Prepare the Broth first. Combine all the ingredients in a saucepan except the tamari or soy sauce and barley malt.

☐ Let simmer for 30 minutes, covered. The Broth is done when the spices and flavorings are well blended.

☐ Strain the finished Broth through a fine sieve. Add the tamari or soy sauce and barley malt. Makes 1 cup.

STIR-FRY

2 cloves garlic, minced
2 large carrots, julienned
1 sweet bell pepper, julienned
2 bunches of scallions, cut into 1- to 2-inch pieces
1 cup snow peas, cleaned and deveined
½ pound asparagus or broccoli, cut into 1- to 2-inch pieces
*   (enough for 1 cup)*
½ cup roasted walnut halves (see roasting instructions on
*   page 21)*
½ pound udon noodles
1 medium eggplant, cut into 1- to 1½-inch cubes
1 egg
cornstarch or arrowroot for rolling eggplant
vegetable oil, enough for ½ inch in bottom of pan
1 tablespoon cornstarch or arrowroot
1 cup Broth
2 tablespoons toasted sesame oil
1 heaping tablespoon peeled and chopped ginger root

☐ Prepare the vegetables. Roast the walnut halves.

☐ Put water on to boil for noodles. Put noodles into boiling water 1 or 2 minutes before starting to stir-fry the vegetables. The noodles will cook in 8 to 10 minutes. When the udon noodles are cooked, remove them from the heat and drain them well. Set aside until ready to serve.

☐ In a medium mixing bowl, beat the egg. Dip the eggplant cubes in the beaten egg, and then roll them in cornstarch.

☐ Deep-fry eggplant cubes in ½ inch hot vegetable oil until browned and tender. Set aside on a paper towel.

☐ Dissolve 1 tablespoon cornstarch or arrowroot in ¼ cup of the Broth.

☐ Heat the toasted sesame oil in the wok so that it is extremely hot. While stir-frying use a medium-high heat.

☐ Stir-fry the carrots, sweet pepper, and asparagus first. When they are partially cooked (in about 2 minutes), add the chopped ginger, garlic, and scallions. Stir-fry another 2 minutes.

☐ When all of the vegetables are on the verge of being done, add the Broth. When the Broth is hot, stir in the cornstarch that was dissolved in ¼ cup Broth.

☐ Add the eggplant, walnuts, and pea pods. Stir until the vegetables are coated with sauce. Cover the wok and let the Broth thicken and the vegetables cook for 1 more minute.

☐ Turn off the heat and serve immediately. Pile udon noodles on each plate and ladle vegetables and Broth onto the noodles. Serves 4.

STIR-FRYING

Stir-frying is a quick method of cooking vegetables, retaining the vegetables' colors and crispness. Because the vegetables cook so quickly, you must have all the ingredients ready before you begin cooking.

The first step then is to cut up the vegetables and prepare any broth or seasoning you will use. Arrange the ingredients near your wok so you can reach them easily when you need them. When everything is ready, place the wok over a burner set on high heat. When the wok is hot, add the oil. When the oil is hot, add the first vegetable directed in the recipe. Add the slower-cooking vegetables first, ending with those that take only seconds.

Stir with chopsticks or a long-handled spoon to keep the food moving so that it cooks evenly and does not stick. To add a broth with a thickening agent such as cornstarch or arrowroot, push the vegetables up the sides of the wok, leaving the center clear of food. Pour the liquid into the center and stir constantly until thickened. Stir all of the ingredients together to heat through. Serve at once to preserve the fresh color and flavor of the vegetables.

Winter Vegetable Pie

This pie has a smooth and creamy texture. Top it with crunchy roasted walnuts for a nice finishing touch. The rich root vegetables combined with tahini and basil create a unique taste for a vegetable pie.

Serve it with a green vegetable and a crisp apple or citrus salad. For a healthy meal add kasha or wild rice

> 1 large leek, diced (or 1½ cups diced onion)
> 1 tablespoon toasted sesame oil
> 4 cups mixed diced carrots, squash, and parsnips
> ½ teaspoon salt
> ½ cup water
> 1 large egg
> pepper to taste
> 1½ teaspoons chopped fresh basil
> ½ cup soy milk or cream
> 2 tablespoons tahini
> 1 9-inch pie shell
> ½ cup coarsely chopped, roasted walnuts (see roasting
>   instructions on page 21)

☐ Sauté leek in toasted sesame oil over moderate flame in a frying pan for approximately 3 minutes.

☐ Add diced vegetables and continue to sauté for 3 more minutes. Add salt and ½ cup water. Simmer, covered, for 15 minutes over medium-low heat until vegetables are soft. Drain off any excess liquid.

☐ Preheat oven to 425°.

☐ Place vegetables, egg, pepper, basil, soy milk or cream, and tahini in a food processor or blender, and purée until creamy. Pour into pie crust, and top with roasted walnuts.

☐ Bake for 10 minutes. Then reduce heat to 350°, and bake for 20 more minutes or until center is firm.

☐ Serves 6.

Butternut Squash and Vegetable Gratin Topped with Roasted Walnuts and Gruyère Cheese

When fall comes, this is one of the first meals I make. I feel fortunate to have a good market where I can go and fill my trunk with a variety of squash from one of my favorite growers. Everyone calls her the "potato lady" because she grows many varieties of potatoes, but I call her the "squash lady." This gratin is nice served with wild rice, salad, and fresh bread.

1 medium butternut squash
olive oil for brushing squash
salt and pepper
2 tablespoons olive oil
6 cloves garlic, minced
2 cups halved and sliced leeks
1 red bell pepper, julienned
3 cups sliced mushrooms (wild mushrooms are great if
  available)
6 to 8 tomatoes, sliced
salt to taste
¼ cup chopped fresh herbs (a mixture of any of these: basil,
  marjoram, parsley, rosemary, thyme, mint, sage)
½ teaspoon salt
½ teaspoon pepper
¾ cup roasted walnuts (see roasting instructions on page 21)
1 cup grated Gruyère or soy cheese

☐ Peel squash and slice into ¼- to ½-inch strips. Lightly brush the strips with olive oil, then sprinkle with salt and pepper. Bake on a cookie sheet at 375° for about 15 minutes, or until almost tender.

☐ Sauté garlic, leeks, and red bell pepper for 5 minutes over medium flame in ½ tablespoon olive oil. Set aside.

☐ Sauté mushrooms in remaining 1½ tablespoons olive oil over medium flame for 5 minutes or until golden brown, stirring frequently. Lightly salt. Set aside.

☐ Layer ingredients in a baking dish (approximately 8 x 11) in the following order: squash, mushrooms, leek-pepper garlic mixture, tomatoes, herbs, salt, pepper, walnuts, and cheese.

☐ Preheat oven to 350°. Bake, covered, for 30 minutes and uncovered for 10 minutes.

☐ Serves 4.

PEELING PUMPKINS AND WINTER SQUASH

To peel a pumpkin or squash, cut off the top and the bottom so it will sit well on a cutting surface. Then cut down the sides, cutting away the skin from the top to the bottom. Cut pumpkin or squash in half and clean out the seeds and stringy pulp. Cut the flesh into chunks for cooking. For butternut squash, cut the bulbous end off of the long cylindrical end and peel each piece separately.

Millet-Almond Loaf

Millet is a grain that is not often used in this country. It is a staple to many people in Africa and other areas where it is hard to cultivate other grains. It is a small grain, looking much like a seed, and contains 10 to 13 percent protein. Millet is usually ground and roasted and made into porridges. We like it for its nutty taste. It is somewhat sticky, which works well for loaves and croquettes.

This loaf goes well with many of our sauces. Try it with the Orange-Shallot (page 192), Ginger-Mushroom (page 188), or Roasted Onion–Miso sauce (page 196). We serve Millet-Almond Loaf with stir-fried broccoli and cauliflower or a mixed greens and tangy fruit salad.

1 cup millet
½ teaspoon salt
3 cups water or Vegetable Stock (see recipe on page 44)
2 tablespoons vegetable oil
½ cup minced onion, firmly packed
½ cup grated parsnip
½ cup minced celery
½ cup grated carrot
salt to taste
1 large egg (optional)
1 tablespoon parsley, minced
½ tablespoon soy sauce or tamari
1 teaspoon dried basil (or 1 tablespoon chopped fresh basil)
¾ cup ground or sliced roasted almonds (see roasting
*   instructions on page 21)*

☐ Roast the millet over medium-high heat in a heavy saucepan. Cook for approximately 3 to 5 minutes or until it begins to pop slightly. Roasting the millet lends a nutty flavor.
☐ Add salt and water or stock. Bring to a boil. Reduce heat, and simmer, covered, approximately 20 to 25 minutes or until the millet has absorbed all the water and is tender.

☐ Sauté the onion for 1 minute in 2 tablespoons vegetable oil. Add parsnips, celery, and carrots, and sauté for 2 to 3 minutes. Salt lightly. Turn off the heat.

☐ In a large bowl, mix together the cooked millet, sautéed vegetables, egg, parsley, soy sauce or tamari, basil, and almonds.

☐ Place mixture into an oiled loaf pan and cover. Bake at 350° for 40 minutes. Uncover for last 5 to 10 minutes.

☐ Remove from oven and let it sit for 10 minutes before turning out of the pan. To unmold loaf, run a knife around the edge, then invert pan on a platter.

☐ Serves 6.

Vietnamese Warm Tempeh Salad

This is a wonderful entrée salad that is substantial enough for a cold winter night. Tempeh is a grain cake made from one or more fermented grains. Tempeh readily soaks up the spices and flavors of a marinade, and sautéing the cake creates a crisp outside. This salad can also be made with mock duck or shrimp.

MARINATED TEMPEH

1½ tablespoons toasted sesame oil
6 cloves garlic, minced
1½ tablespoons peeled and minced ginger root
¼ cup mirin
¼ cup tamari or soy sauce
3 tablespoons orange juice
1 8-ounce package of tempeh

☐ In a hot skillet with 1½ tablespoons toasted sesame oil, briefly sauté garlic and ginger, stirring well. Do not burn. Add mirin, tamari or soy sauce, and 2 tablespoons of the orange juice.
☐ Place whole block of tempeh in the marinade. Cover and simmer for 5 minutes on each side. Remove tempeh and set aside, and save marinade in a bowl. Add 1 tablespoon of the orange juice to the marinade to thin. Use this as a sauce for the noodles.

VEGETABLES

1 heaping cup julienned carrots
1 heaping cup deveined pea pods
1 cucumber, peeled and sliced
1 tomato, cut in wedges (optional)
lettuce, washed and trimmed
½ pound rice stick noodles or vermicelli
pinch of salt
1 tablespoon vegetable oil

Toasted Sesame Vinaigrette (see recipe on page 22)
1 bunch scallions, sliced on the diagonal; roasted peanuts (see
page 21 for roasting instructions); and chopped fresh
cilantro or mint for garnish

☐ Prepare all the vegetables.

☐ Boil water with pinch of salt for the noodles (follow package directions for quantity). Before boiling noodles, blanch the carrots and pea pods in this water: First drop in the julienned carrots. Leave them in for 2 minutes, remove with a slotted spoon, and run them under cold water until cool. Repeat the procedure with the pea pods, but leave them in for only about 30 seconds.

☐ Drop the noodles into the boiling water and cook for approximately 6 minutes. Drain. Do not rinse with water. Cool.

☐ In a hot skillet with 1 tablespoon vegetable oil, sauté marinated tempeh until golden brown on each side. Cut tempeh into 9 pieces.

☐ To serve: Dress lettuce with Sesame Vinaigrette. Place some lettuce on each serving plate. Top with chilled noodles. Pour leftover marinade on the noodles. Surround the noodles with carrots, pea pods, cucumber, and tomato wedges. Top the noodles with tempeh. Garnish with scallions, peanuts, and cilantro or mint. Serves 3.

TEMPEH

Tempeh was originally made in Indonesia. It is made from a variety of fermented grains, legumes, and sea vegetables in many different combinations. Tempeh is very high in protein, calcium, and vitamin B_{12}.

Tempeh is sold as a frozen cake. It absorbs flavors well, even though it has a unique nutty taste of its own. Use marinated tempeh in salads, stir-fries, or grilled on kabobs. Sliced tempeh can be sautéed and made into vegetarian Reuben sandwiches, tempeh burgers, or crumbled and formed into croquettes with other grains and vegetables.

North African Couscous-Vegetable Pilaf with Harissa Sauce

Serve this pilaf with Cucumber-Dill Soup (page 48) or a cucumber-yogurt salad. Try dates and tea for a simple dessert.

COUSCOUS

2 cups couscous
2 cups water
½ teaspoon salt
pinch of saffron

☐ Over moderate heat, briefly dry-roast couscous in sauté pan until lightly browned, approximately 5 minutes.

☐ In a separate saucepan, combine water, salt, and saffron. Bring to a boil. Carefully pour the water into the couscous pan and cover. Let sit for 15 minutes, or until couscous absorbs all of the water. Transfer the couscous to a bowl and fluff with a fork.

NORTH AFRICAN COUSCOUS-VEGETABLE PILAF

½ cup dried chickpeas
4 cups water for soaking
6 cups water for cooking
2 to 3 cups diced winter squash or yams
1½ cups halved green beans
2½ tablespoons olive oil
1 tablespoon minced garlic
1 cup chopped leeks or onions
1 cup chopped fresh bulb fennel, zucchini, or sweet bell
  pepper
2 cups couscous, cooked

¼ teaspoon allspice
1 teaspoon fennel seeds
1 teaspoon turmeric
¼ teaspoon ground coriander
¼ teaspoon cumin
½ cup plumped or moist raisins
½ to ¾ cup roasted almonds (see roasting instructions on
*   page 21)*
salt to taste
1 cup diced tomato
roasted almonds for garnish
Harissa Sauce (optional; see recipe on page 138)

☐ Soak chickpeas in 4 cups water for at least 4 hours or overnight.

☐ Drain the chickpeas, rinse, and cover with 6 cups water. Bring to a boil, reduce the heat, and simmer, covered, for 1½ hours or until done. Drain.

☐ Steam the diced squash or yams for 7 to 10 minutes until just soft.

☐ Blanch the green beans: Plunge them into boiling water, and cook for 3 to 5 minutes. Remove from the heat, strain, and rinse with cold water to cool.

☐ In a large pan, sauté garlic, leeks or onions, and fennel (or zucchini or pepper) in 2 tablespoons olive oil for approximately 3 minutes.

☐ Add chickpeas, green beans, couscous, seasonings, raisins, almonds, and salt. Continue to sauté over low heat, stirring gently, until all the contents are heated through.

☐ In another pan, sauté tomatoes and steamed squash in remaining ½ tablespoon olive oil just until hot.

☐ Mound couscous mixture on a large platter with the squash and tomatoes in the center. Garnish with roasted almonds.

☐ Serve with Harissa Sauce. Serves 6.

Shepherd's Pie

This can be a seasonal dish and uses whatever vegetables are available. Corn, squash, and green beans name just a few that are great substitutes. It's also a good way to use leftover potatoes. Serve Shepherd's Pie with a green salad.

3 cups peeled and cubed potatoes
1½ cups peeled and cubed rutabaga (you may use a total of
    4½ cups potatoes instead of using any rutabaga)
3 cups water
1½ teaspoons salt
2 tablespoons butter
¼ cup heavy cream (optional)
3 tablespoons olive oil
2 cups diced leeks
3 to 5 cloves garlic, minced
¾ cup peeled and sliced carrot
½ cup white wine
1 medium red bell pepper, diced
2 ribs celery, sliced
1 cup sliced mushrooms (use fresh shiitake, crimini, or
    button)
salt to taste
¾ cup diced tomato
1 cup fresh or frozen peas (optional)
2 cups cleaned, destemmed, and chopped spinach (or 1 cup
    chopped cabbage)
½ teaspoon paprika
pepper to taste
1 tablespoon chopped fresh herbs: basil, thyme, or sage (or ½
    tablespoon dried herbs)
a few dashes Tabasco™

☐ Cover potatoes and rutabagas with 3 cups water, add 1 teaspoon of the salt, and bring to a boil. Reduce the heat, and simmer, covered, for 20 minutes. Drain, reserving the cooking liquid.

☐ Whip the potatoes and rutabagas with 2 tablespoons butter and ¼ cup of the reserved potato cooking water or cream.

☐ Over a medium flame, sauté leeks and garlic with 2 tablespoons olive oil for 4 minutes. Add carrots, and sauté for another 2 minutes. Add the wine, and cover the skillet. Cook for 2 minutes, then remove the skillet from the heat and transfer the cooked vegetables to a large bowl. Set aside.

☐ Preheat oven to 400°.

☐ Over medium heat, sauté for about 3 minutes the bell pepper, celery, and mushrooms in the remaining 1 tablespoon olive oil (if you are using cabbage, also add it now). Salt lightly. Add tomatoes, and peas (if you are using the spinach, add it now). Cover the skillet and cook for 2 minutes. Add these vegetables to the leek mixture.

☐ Gently mix vegetables. Add remaining ½ teaspoon salt. Add paprika, pepper, and herbs, and sprinkle with Tabasco™.

☐ Mix together and spoon into a 2½-quart casserole, or divide among individual gratin dishes. Top the vegetables with the whipped potatoes. For a nice effect, pipe potatoes onto the vegetables with a pastry bag, using a large tip.

☐ Bake covered for 10 minutes, then remove cover and bake for 15 to 20 minutes. Potatoes should be light brown on top when done.

☐ Serves 4 to 6.

Baked, Stuffed Squash with Leek-Orange Sauce

Baked, Stuffed Squash with Leek-Orange Sauce was inspired by a meal at Omen in New York. It is a nutritious and filling entrée. Serve with a steamed green vegetable and rice.

LEEK-ORANGE SAUCE

2½ cups chopped leeks
1 tablespoon vegetable oil
2 cups water
2 tablespoons orange juice concentrate
1½ tablespoons white miso
salt to taste

☐ Sauté leeks in 1 tablespoon vegetable oil over medium heat, for approximately 5 minutes. Add water and orange juice. Cover and bring to boil.
☐ Turn down the heat and simmer, covered, for 10 minutes until the leeks are very tender. Add the miso and salt. Blend until very smooth in a blender or food processor. Serve warm.

BAKED, STUFFED SQUASH

2 acorn squash
1 teaspoon toasted sesame or vegetable oil
1 onion, diced
1 parsnip, diced
1 rib celery, diced
1 tablespoon mirin or water
¾ pound (preferably soft) tofu, crumbled
½ cup cooked (follow package directions) and chopped hijiki
     or arame seaweed (optional)
½ cup chopped, roasted walnuts (see roasting instructions on
     page 21)
1 teaspoon peeled and grated ginger root
½ tablespoon tamari or soy sauce

☐ Prebake squash. Cut them in half, and clean out the seeds. Bake in 350° oven with cut side down in a baking dish with a little water for approximately 35 to 45 minutes. When a fork pierces the flesh easily and the squash is almost done, remove from the oven.

☐ Increase heat in oven to 400°.

☐ Pour sesame or vegetable oil in a skillet. Heat oil, and add the onion. Sauté for 1 minute, stirring. Add the parsnip and continue to stir for another 2 to 3 minutes. Add celery, reduce the heat to medium-low, and sauté an additional 2 to 3 minutes.

☐ Add mirin or water, cover, and cook over low heat for a few more minutes until all vegetables are tender.

☐ Combine sautéed vegetables, tofu, seaweed, walnuts, ginger, and tamari or soy sauce in a bowl. Stir until well combined.

☐ Fill prebaked squash cavities with vegetable mixture, and bake in a low baking dish, covered, for approximately 15 minutes or until squash is heated thoroughly.

☐ Serve alone or with Leek-Orange Sauce. Serves 4.

Croquettes

Croquettes are very versatile. Made of grains and vegetables, they can easily be a light lunch or a hearty dinner entrée, and they can be served plain or with a sauce. Ours are combinations of grains, vegetables, spices, and often nuts, that are mixed together and formed into patties. Fried in a little oil, they become crisp cakes. The combinations are endless.

Once you have tried some of our suggestions and mastered the required consistency and cooking methods, you will have discovered a new use for grains and a great way to use up leftover potatoes and grains.

Croquettes should be somewhat sticky to hold together while cooking. Here are some suggestions for getting the mixture to hold together:

☐ If you are using leftover grains, steam them first to put some moisture back into them.

☐ Another method to try, whether you have added an egg or not, is to put half of the croquette mixture in a food processor or grinder. Process for 30 to 60 seconds, add the ground mixture back to the remaining mixture, and stir well to combine. This step develops the gluten in the grains, helping to bind the ingredients together. Do not process too much. You want some texture left in the croquette mixture.

☐ Add an egg if your mixture seems dry and does not hold together when you press it in your hand.

☐ To avoid problems while forming croquettes, start with clean hands, and rinse your hands often. If your hands are slightly wet, the mixture won't stick to them as much.

☐ When forming the croquettes it is important to be firm and really compress them. If they are not pressed together well, they will fall apart while cooking.

☐ When cooking the croquettes, use a hot skillet with enough oil to coat the bottom of the pan. You do not need a lot of oil. Do not crowd them in the pan; leave space between them. Cook one side of the patty until it is golden brown, and turn only once. They tend to break apart with any extra handling.

If you have leftover croquette mixture, form it into patties before refrigerating. They will keep for several days when well wrapped.

Buckwheat-Potato with Ginger-Mushroom Sauce

These are very hearty croquettes for fall and winter. They'll keep you warm and strong. Serve Buckwheat-Potato Croquettes with Ginger-Mushroom Sauce, steamed cauliflower, broccoli or greens, and either Cranberry-Fruit Salad (page 38) or an apple salad.

GINGER-MUSHROOM SAUCE

½ ounce dried shiitake mushrooms, soaked in warm water
    for 30 minutes and sliced
4 cups water (include the water used for soaking mushrooms)
1 large onion, sliced
1 medium carrot, sliced
5 cloves garlic, smashed
1 tablespoon star anise
¼ cup chopped ginger root
½ teaspoon salt
1 tablespoon toasted sesame oil
1½ cups sliced button mushrooms
1 to 2 tablespoons tamari or soy sauce
2½ tablespoons cornstarch or arrowroot
¼ cup water for dissolving cornstarch

☐ Prepare *shiitake* mushrooms, reserving soaking water.

☐ To make the stock: Combine water, onion, carrot, garlic, anise, ginger, and salt in a saucepan. Bring to a boil, and then lower the heat. Simmer stock, covered, 20 minutes over low heat. Strain.

☐ Sauté button and *shiitake* mushrooms in the sesame oil for 3 to 5 minutes. Add to the strained stock. Add tamari or soy sauce. Dissolve cornstarch or arrowroot in a little water and stir into sauce. Bring to a boil, stirring often, until sauce thickens.

CROQUETTES

1½ cups buckwheat groats
3½ cups water
1 teaspoon salt
1 small onion, minced
1 tablespoon toasted sesame or vegetable oil
1 stalk celery, minced
1 small carrot, minced
2 small to medium potatoes, cubed very small (should have 2
    cups)
¼ cup tahini
2 tablespoons chopped parsley
¼ cup finely chopped scallions
2½ tablespoons tamari or soy sauce
vegetable oil for sautéing

☐ Dry-roast buckwheat groats in heavy skillet over medium-low heat. Cook for 10 to 12 minutes, stirring frequently.

☐ Add 3½ cups water and 1 teaspoon of salt to groats. Cover, and cook over low heat until water is gone and groats are cooked, approximately 20 to 25 minutes.

☐ Sauté onion in 1 tablespoon toasted sesame or vegetable oil until translucent. Add celery and carrot, and sauté for 3 to 5 minutes or until vegetables are soft.

☐ Blanch potatoes until done, about 5 minutes. Drain.

☐ Combine groats, sautéed vegetables, potatoes, and remaining ingredients. Let cool enough to handle.

☐ Form into 2-inch patties. In a large frying pan over medium heat, sauté croquettes in vegetable oil until crispy and golden brown. Turn patties over, and cook until crispy and golden on the other side.

☐ Makes twelve 2-inch croquettes. Serves 6.

Chickpea-Vegetable with Tahini-Vegetable Sauce

These croquettes are somewhat similar to the Middle Eastern falafel balls. They are wonderful and refreshing when topped with the Tahini-Vegetable Sauce. We enjoy them most when served with couscous or pita bread and steamed vegetables such as green beans or cauliflower, or grilled eggplant. Olives are a must!

TAHINI-VEGETABLE SAUCE

1 cup tahini
½ cup water
juice of 2 lemons
3 cloves garlic, finely chopped
2 tablespoons chopped fresh parsley
½ teaspoon salt
½ cucumber, peeled, seeded, and diced
1 cup diced tomato

☐ In a blender, mix together tahini, water, and lemon juice until smooth.
☐ In a bowl, combine tahini mixture, garlic, parsley, salt, diced cucumbers, and tomatoes. You may need to adjust water and lemon juice to get a nice sauce consistency, depending on the kind of tahini you use.
☐ Serve slightly chilled.

TAHINI

Tahini is a paste or "butter" made from ground raw sesame seeds. Tahini made from roasted sesame seeds is called sesame butter, and has a strong nutty flavor. Tahini is a staple in many of the eastern Mediterranean countries, where it is found in many sauces and often paired with chickpeas. It will keep almost indefinitely in a glass jar in the refrigerator.

CROQUETTES

6 cups water for soaking
6 cups water for cooking
1½ cups dried chickpeas
1½ tablespoons olive oil
1 small onion, minced
1 carrot, grated
3 cloves garlic, crushed
1 stalk celery, minced
½ teaspoon turmeric
1½ teaspoons ground coriander
1 teaspoon paprika
¼ teaspoon cayenne
1½ teaspoons salt
1 egg, beaten
vegetable oil for sautéing
bread crumbs

☐ In 6 cups water, soak chickpeas overnight or for at least 3 hours. Drain chickpeas, discarding soaking liquid.

☐ In a large pot, cover chickpeas with 6 cups water. Bring them to a boil, and then lower heat. Let chickpeas simmer, covered, until tender, approximately 1½ hours. Check them occasionally to see if they need more water.

☐ Drain and mash chickpeas when tender. A food processor works well, or mash them by hand.

☐ Sauté onion, carrot, garlic, and celery in olive oil for 3 to 5 minutes over medium heat.

☐ Combine mashed chickpeas, sautéed vegetables, spices, salt, and egg. Stir well. If mixture is too wet, add up to ½ cup bread crumbs.

☐ Form croquettes, making them about 2 inches in diameter. Sauté in hot vegetable oil until well-browned on both sides.

☐ Serve with Tahini-Vegetable Sauce. Makes 12 croquettes.

Couscous-Almond with Orange-Shallot Sauce

Couscous is a delicious, light North African grain made from wheat. Try these croquettes with different sauces. For a spicy version, serve with Harissa Sauce (page 138), or try the tangy Orange-Shallot Sauce. Serve with green beans, grilled eggplant, and olives.

Orange-Shallot Sauce is also good on grilled or broiled fish. We often use wine in making this, but it is not necessary. Simply increase the quantity of orange juice if you prefer a simple citrus sauce.

ORANGE-SHALLOT SAUCE

2 tablespoons butter or olive oil
½ cup minced shallots
¾ cup white wine (optional)
1½ cups orange juice (preferably fresh squeezed)
3 bay leaves
¼ teaspoon salt
1½ tablespoons cornstarch or arrowroot
¼ cup cold water
1 tablespoon chopped fresh chives
grated orange rind to taste (optional)

☐ Sauté shallots over medium heat in 2 tablespoons butter or oil for approximately 3 minutes until shallots become translucent.

☐ Add wine, orange juice, bay leaves, and salt. (Use 2 cups of orange juice if you are omitting the wine.) Bring to a boil, and then turn down and simmer a few minutes.

☐ Mix the cornstarch or arrowroot and cold water together and whisk into the simmering sauce. Pull out bay leaves, and add chives. If the sauce seems to need more orange flavor, add a little grated orange rind. Makes 2½ cups.

CROQUETTES

1½ cups couscous
1½ teaspoons salt
½ teaspoon anise seed
⅓ cup currants
3 cups water or Vegetable Stock (see recipe on page 44)
1 tablespoon olive oil
1 onion, minced
3 cloves garlic, minced
2 carrots, grated
1 stalk celery, minced
1 egg, lightly beaten
1 tablespoon chopped parsley or mint
¼ teaspoon cayenne
½ cup sliced, roasted almonds (see roasting instructions on
     page 21)
peanut or vegetable oil for sautéing

☐ In a saucepan over medium-high flame, dry-roast the couscous, stirring constantly for approximately 3 to 5 minutes until couscous smells toasty.

☐ Add salt, anise seed, currants, and water or stock to couscous. Use caution when adding water to a hot saucepan! Stir, and cover immediately. Turn heat to medium-high for 2 to 3 minutes while couscous comes to a boil. Turn heat off, and leave pan covered for 10 minutes.

☐ Sauté onions and garlic for 1 minute in 1 tablespoon olive oil. Add carrots and celery, and continue to sauté for 2 to 3 minutes more.

☐ In a large bowl, mix together the beaten egg, cooked couscous mixture, sautéed vegetables, parsley or mint, cayenne, and roasted almonds.

☐ Shape the couscous mixture firmly into 3-inch patties. Sauté in peanut or vegetable oil until crispy and light brown on both sides. Makes 12 croquettes.

Basmati Rice, Red Bean, and Vegetable with Salsa

These croquettes are made with Basmati rice, which makes them very light and crispy. The pumpkin seeds add a nice flavor, but you could substitute sunflower seeds. An avocado-cucumber salad and steamed vegetables such as green beans or sweet corn are good accompaniments. Top the croquettes with salsa.

SALSA

½ cup finely chopped onion
1 red bell pepper, finely diced
1 green bell pepper, finely diced
2 cups finely diced tomato (fresh or canned)
3 jalapeños, minced
1 small head of garlic, minced
2 tablespoons cilantro, chopped
juice of ½ lemon
juice of 1 lime
2 tablespoons olive oil
salt to taste
cayenne pepper (optional)

☐ Combine all ingredients, adding cayenne or more jalapeño to taste. The flavor of this salsa improves as it sits, so make it in the morning or the day before serving. Makes 3 cups.

CROQUETTES

½ cup small dried red beans
4 cups water
2 cups Basmati rice
2¾ cups water
½ teaspoon salt
½ tablespoon vegetable oil
¾ cup minced red, yellow, or green onion
2 medium carrots, grated
1 stalk celery, minced
1 egg (optional)
½ cup coarsely chopped, roasted pumpkin seeds (see roasting
    instructions on page 155)
½ teaspoon ground cumin
½ teaspoon ground coriander
salt and pepper to taste
vegetable oil for sautéing

☐ Wash beans. Cover them with 4 cups water and bring to a boil, and then reduce the heat and simmer, covered, until beans are soft, approximately 50 minutes.

☐ Cover rice with 2¾ cups of water and add ½ teaspoon salt. Bring the rice to a boil, and then cover the pan and reduce the heat and simmer until rice is done, about 25 minutes.

☐ In a hot skillet, sauté onion, carrot, and celery until tender in ½ tablespoon vegetable oil.

☐ Combine rice, beans, carrots, celery, and onion in a large bowl. Add egg, pumpkin seeds, spices, and salt and pepper. Mix well.

☐ Form into 2- to 3-inch patties, pressing hard so they stay together. If your hands are dry, the mixture will stick to them. Keep water or vegetable oil on your hands while you form the patties.

☐ Sauté croquettes in vegetable oil until golden brown on both sides. It is best to handle them as little as possible. Flip them only once, and avoid pushing them around. Do not crowd the pan.

☐ Makes 12 croquettes.

Brown Rice, Almond, and Vegetable with Roasted Onion–Miso Sauce

This is a great way to use leftover rice, but there is a trick to getting it to stick together. Leftover rice is often dry, and we have found that it helps to steam it. If it is still not sticky enough, grind some of it up (as suggested in the croquette introduction).

Try replacing the almonds with a variety of chopped nuts: They all work well and each adds its distinct flavor. Serve with squash and a mixed green and vegetable salad.

ROASTED ONION–MISO SAUCE

6 medium onions
1 bulb garlic
2 tablespoons white miso
1 tablespoon red miso
¼ cup mirin
2 tablespoons barley malt
salt to taste
½ to 1 cup water or Vegetable Stock (see recipe on page 44)

☐ Preheat oven to 425°.
☐ Place whole onions and garlic on a baking sheet in the oven. Bake them for 45 minutes and remove garlic. Continue to bake the onions approximately 15 more minutes or until they soften. If you are using small onions, 45 minutes will probably be enough for them too. Remove the onion and garlic from the oven. Let garlic and onions cool down enough so you can peel them.
☐ Put the peeled onions, garlic, miso, mirin, malt, and salt in a blender, and purée. Add as much water or stock as necessary for a sauce consistency.
☐ Serve warm.

CROQUETTES

1½ cups short grain brown rice
3½ cups water
1 teaspoon salt
¾ cup roasted, slivered almonds
1 tablespoon vegetable oil
½ cup minced celery
¾ cup grated parsnips
¾ cup grated sweet potatoes or carrots
¾ cup minced green onion
⅓ cup chopped fresh parsley
1 tablespoon tamari
1 egg, beaten
vegetable oil for sautéing

☐ In a saucepan, bring rice, water, and salt to a boil. Cover pan, and turn down heat to a low simmer. Cook for approximately 45 minutes, until all the water has been absorbed. Set aside to cool slightly.

☐ Roast almonds in oven for 15 minutes at 350°.

☐ In a large skillet, heat vegetable oil. Add celery, parsnips, and sweet potatoes or carrots. Sauté over medium heat for a few minutes. Add green onions, and sauté for 1 more minute.

☐ In a large bowl, mix together vegetables, parsley, tamari, egg, almonds, and rice.

☐ Form into 3-inch patties. Sauté in vegetable oil in a large skillet until golden brown on both sides. Makes 16 croquettes.

Roasted Eggplant Patties with Tomato-Basil Sauce

Roasted eggplant has a rich, smoky flavor that blends well with fresh mint. Serve on a bed of pasta that you have tossed with olive oil, parsley, salt, and pepper. Add a green vegetable to complete the meal.

TOMATO-BASIL SAUCE

12 large Roma tomatoes (or 10 regular tomatoes)
2 tablespoons olive oil
6 cloves garlic, minced
2 tablespoons chopped fresh basil
salt and pepper to taste

☐ Blanch tomatoes: Drop tomatoes into boiling water for 10 seconds. Peel, seed, and finely chop.
☐ Sauté garlic in olive oil. Add chopped tomatoes, fresh basil, and salt and pepper. Simmer together for 5 minutes, and serve over croquettes.

CROQUETTES

CROQUETTES

2 to 3 medium-sized eggplants
4 tablespoons olive oil
1 cup finely diced onion
½ cup finely grated Parmesan cheese
½ cup bread crumbs
1 large egg
1 tablespoon chopped mint
1 tablespoon chopped parsley
salt and pepper to taste

☐ Roast the whole eggplant directly over flames on stove, turning until charred evenly on all sides (approximately 5 minutes). The eggplant's center meat should be soft. If you are using large eggplants, you can finish cooking them in the oven: Place whole eggplant in a 400° oven until the eggplant is soft in the center. The eggplant will feel soft and can be pierced easily with a fork. Let the eggplant cool until you can touch it, peel it, and finely chop the meat. You should have 3½ cups of chopped eggplant meat.

☐ Sauté the diced onion in 1 tablespoon of the olive oil for 3 to 5 minutes.

☐ Mix all ingredients together; chill for approximately 45 minutes. The mixture will not be really firm, but it should hold together when sautéed. If it is too loose, add a few more bread crumbs.

☐ Gently shape the mixture into 2-inch patties, and gently dip them in flour. Sauté the patties in the remaining 3 tablespoons olive oil until golden brown.

☐ Serve with Tomato-Basil Sauce. Makes 12 croquettes.

Butternut Squash, Cheese, and Walnut

These croquettes are very appealing on a cool fall day, and they can be made with other varieties of winter squash. We like to serve these with Tomato-Basil Sauce (recipe page 198), a crisp romaine salad, and hearty bread such as Hearty Wheat (page 84) or Pumpernickel Rye (page 90) spread with Roasted Garlic.

1 medium butternut squash
1 bunch scallions, minced
¾ cup finely chopped, roasted walnuts
1 apple, grated (any cooking apple will do)
¾ cup grated cheese (Gouda, baby Swiss, or soy mozzarella)
2 eggs, beaten
1 tablespoon chopped parsley
½ teaspoon salt
½ teaspoon pepper
vegetable or olive oil for sautéing

☐ Peel squash (see instructions on page 175), and cut into large chunks. Steam lightly for 7 minutes, or until squash still has some crispness but is beginning to soften. Set aside to cool, and then grate 3 cups of the squash.
☐ Roast walnuts at 350° for 15 minutes.
☐ Mix all ingredients together in a large bowl.
☐ Form mixture into patties 2-inch in diameter. In a large frying pan, sauté croquettes in vegetable or olive oil until crispy and golden brown.
☐ Note: Serve the Tomato-Basil Sauce on the side so the croquettes remain crispy. Serves 4.

ROASTING GARLIC

To roast garlic, place a whole, unpeeled garlic head in a preheated 400° oven, and roast it for approximately 30 minutes or until the head is very soft. Remove the garlic from the oven, and set it aside to cool slightly.

Remove the outer papery peel; with large heads, it is easiest to remove the cloves on the side and peel those individually. Slice off about ¼ to ½ inch of the bottom of the cloves to "open" them. Holding on to the top of the cloves, squeeze the roasted garlic pulp from the cloves into a bowl.

Serve the roasted pulp as a spread for bread.

Tofu, Vegetable, and Peanut with Sweet and Sour Sauce

These croquettes are easy and nutritious. Serve them on a bed of rice covered with Sweet and Sour Sauce, and steamed vegetables. Another fun way to serve them is on a bun with ketchup, pickles, and coleslaw, and sweet corn.

SWEET AND SOUR SAUCE

> 2 cups water
> 2 cups pineapple-coconut, apple, or pineapple juice
> 1-inch piece ginger root, sliced
> 2 cloves garlic, mashed
> ¼ onion, peeled and chopped
> 2 tablespoons rice wine vinegar
> salt to taste
> 1 tablespoon mirin (optional)
> 1 teaspoon tamari
> 2 tablespoons cornstarch or arrowroot, dissolved in ¼ cup
> cold water

☐ Cover and simmer all the ingredients except cornstarch or arrowroot for 30 minutes. Strain, reserving liquid. Return to the heat. Add the cornstarch mixture, and stir until sauce has thickened slightly.

☐ Optional: Add chunks of fresh pineapple and fresh, peeled tomatoes to the ingredients before simmering.

☐ Makes 4 cups.

CROQUETTES

½ tablespoon vegetable oil
1 large carrot, grated
1 stalk celery, minced
4 scallions, minced
1 package firm tofu
⅓ cup roasted sesame seeds (see instructions on page 78)
⅓ cup chopped peanuts
2 tablespoons tahini
1 tablespoon white miso (optional)
1 tablespoon tamari or soy sauce
salt to taste
black pepper to taste
cayenne to taste
¾ cup bread or cracker crumbs
1 to 2 eggs
vegetable oil for sautéing

☐ Sauté carrot and celery in ½ tablespoon vegetable oil. After a few minutes, add scallions and sauté for 1 more minute.

☐ Mash tofu with a fork. Add remaining ingredients to tofu, and continue mixing until tofu is completely broken up and ingredients are evenly blended. Add a second egg if mixture does not hold together.

☐ Form into 2- to 3-inch croquettes. Sauté in hot vegetable oil. Makes 8 croquettes.

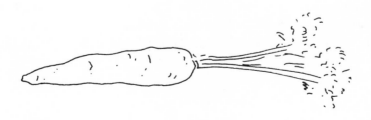

Wild Rice, Vegetable, and Pecan with Wild Mushroom Cream Sauce

Wild Rice, Vegetable, and Pecan Croquettes are very satisfying. This is a good meal to serve to friends or relatives. You can create a rather festive dinner by serving the croquettes with some traditional side dishes such as cranberries, baked squash or root vegetables, and steamed broccoli, cauliflower, or Brussels sprouts. In the summer, serve with marinated vegetables and a Waldorf salad.

WILD MUSHROOM CREAM SAUCE

This sauce is very good made with soy milk, which makes it just as rich as when it is made with milk. For a creamier sauce, purée half of the sauce.

> 2 cups milk, half and half, or soy milk
> 3 tablespoons butter or vegetable oil
> 1 small onion, finely diced
> 2 shallots, minced
> 1½ cups sliced mushrooms
> 4 to 6 dried wild mushrooms, soaked and chopped (optional)
> 2 tablespoons flour
> 1 tablespoon chopped chives (optional)
> salt and pepper to taste

☐ Pour milk (or half and half or soy) in a saucepan, and warm it over low heat. Do not let it scorch or come to a boil. Set it aside.

☐ Sauté onion and shallots in butter or oil for 1 minute. Add mushrooms and continue to sauté for approximately 3 minutes over medium-low heat. Stir in the flour. Cook for 2 to 3 minutes, stirring frequently. Whisk in the warm milk until creamy. Add chives and salt and pepper.

CROQUETTES

½ cup wild rice
½ cup short grain brown rice
2½ cups water
½ teaspoon salt
2 tablespoons vegetable oil
½ cup minced onion
½ cup finely grated carrot
½ cup finely grated parsnip
½ cup minced celery
½ cup finely chopped, roasted pecans (see roasting
    instructions on page 21)
1 egg
2 teaspoons tamari or soy sauce
¼ teaspoon dried thyme
salt and pepper to taste
vegetable oil for sautéing

☐ Wash all the rice thoroughly. Combine the wild and brown rice with 2½ cups of water. Add ½ teaspoon salt. Bring to a boil, boil for 5 minutes, and then reduce heat. Cover pan and simmer for approximately 45 minutes or until rice absorbs all the water.

☐ Sauté onions in 2 tablespoons oil for 2 minutes. Add carrots, parsnips, and celery, and sauté for 5 minutes more.

☐ In a bowl, combine sautéed vegetables, pecans, egg, tamari or soy sauce, seasonings, and rice. Stir until well-mixed. Shape into 3-inch patties.

☐ Sauté patties in hot vegetable oil until crispy and golden brown.

☐ Serve with Wild Mushroom Cream Sauce or Ginger-Mushroom Sauce (page 188). Makes 12 croquettes.

TAMARI
Tamari is the original soy sauce. It is naturally fermented from soybeans and wheat, and can also be wheat-free. Tamari has a richer, more complex flavor than most American-made soy sauces.

Tempeh-Potato with Spicy Peanut Sambal

These are very nice served with a cucumber-mint salad, and try this vegetable dish: spinach, slivered onions, and tomato wedges sautéed in Coconut Milk (recipe page 116) and lime juice with salt, and garnished with roasted cashews or peanuts.

SPICY PEANUT SAMBAL

2 fresh hot green chilies, stemmed and seeded
4 cloves garlic
1 cup roasted peanuts
1 tablespoon soy sauce
2 tablespoons fresh lime juice
3 tablespoons raisins
1 tablespoon honey

☐ Put all ingredients in a food processor and grind into a chunky paste.

CROQUETTES

6 medium to small potatoes (2 cups mashed)
3 tablespoons vegetable oil
1 8-ounce tempeh cake
1½ tablespoons minced garlic
1 teaspoon dried coriander
1 teaspoon dried cumin
1 cup grated carrot
1 cup minced scallion
2 teaspoons salt
fresh ground pepper to taste
1 egg, beaten
2 tablespoons chopped parsley
vegetable oil for sautéing

☐ Peel and boil potatoes until done, approximately 20 minutes. Drain. Mash them and set aside.

☐ Heat 2 tablespoons of the vegetable oil. Cut the tempeh cake into 4 pieces. Sauté the tempeh over medium heat for approximately 3 minutes or until golden brown.

☐ Turn the tempeh, and add garlic, coriander, and cumin. Break up the tempeh pieces with a fork, stirring in the spices to keep them from burning and to help tempeh absorb them.

☐ Turn down the heat to low, and cook for 2 to 3 minutes. Transfer the tempeh-spice mixture to a bowl and set aside. When the mixture is cool, crumble up the tempeh.

☐ Heat the remaining 1 tablespoon of oil. Sauté carrot and scallion for 1 to 2 minutes.

☐ Combine potatoes, tempeh, and sautéed vegetables. Add salt, pepper, egg, and parsley. Stir well.

☐ Form into 3-inch patties. Sauté in vegetable oil until golden brown on both sides.

☐ Serve with Spicy Peanut Sambal on the side. Makes 10 croquettes.

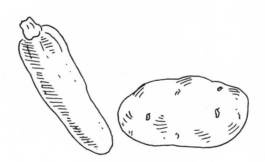

Vegetable Pancakes

These pancakes make a good, simple meal, and kids love them! We like to serve them different ways: sprinkled with soy sauce and served with rice and a steamed vegetable or a salad, or served with applesauce and sour cream. Vegetable Pancakes are also great when served with Apple or Pear Sauce (page 254).

1 large potato, grated (approximately 1½ cups)
3 medium carrots, grated
1 zucchini, grated
1 large parsnip, grated
1 bunch scallions, minced
1 teaspoon salt
3 eggs
pepper to taste
¾ cup unbleached flour
vegetable oil for sautéing

☐ Grate potato, and rinse twice with cold water to remove starch. Squeeze out all excess juice.
☐ Mix all grated vegetables, scallions, and salt. Let sit 10 to 15 minutes to sweat the vegetables.
☐ Separate eggs. Add 3 egg yolks, pepper, and flour to vegetable mixture, and stir well. Beat egg whites until stiff and gently fold into the pancake batter.
☐ Pour the batter into 3- to 4-inch pancakes onto a heavy-bottomed skillet or a griddle, and fry them in very hot oil.
☐ Serves 4 to 6.

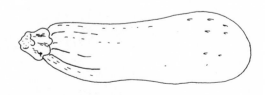

DESSERTS

Almond with Chocolate Ganache

This is a very delicious and versatile cake. We serve it layered with a variety of different fillings: berries and whipped cream, raspberry preserves, Chocolate Ganache, or orange marmalade lightened with whipped cream to name a few. Top with either Chocolate Ganache or whipped cream. Almond Cake is also a delightful base for strawberry shortcake.

ALMOND CAKE

½ cup butter
1 cup honey
3 eggs, separated, plus 1 additional egg white
½ cup plain yogurt
1 teaspoon almond extract
1 cup unbleached white flour
1½ cups ground almonds
1½ teaspoons baking soda
1½ teaspoons baking powder
½ teaspoon salt

☐ Preheat oven to 350°.
☐ Cream butter. Add honey, and beat until creamy. Add 3 egg yolks, yogurt, and almond extract. Beat until well-blended.
☐ Combine flour, ground almonds, baking soda, baking powder, and salt in a separate bowl. Stir dry ingredients into butter mixture.
☐ Whip the 4 egg whites until stiff. Gently fold the egg whites into the batter with a spatula.
☐ Butter and flour two 9-inch cake pans. Pour batter into the 2 pans.

☐ Bake for 25 to 30 minutes. Cake is done when a cake tester inserted in the center comes out clean. Let cool before taking out of pans.

☐ Cool layers completely before filling. Place filling between layers and top with whipped cream or Chocolate Ganache; the Chocolate Ganache will drip down the sides. We leave the sides unfrosted.

CHOCOLATE GANACHE

6 ounces unsweetened chocolate
1 cup heavy cream
½ cup honey
1 teaspoon crème de cacao

☐ Melt chocolate in a double boiler. Remove from the heat, and cool to room temperature.

☐ Warm the cream in a saucepan over low heat until just warm. Do not let it boil.

☐ Stir honey, crème de cacao, and warmed cream into chocolate. Stir gently with a spoon until well-combined. Whisk ganache for about 30 seconds until it lightens in color and looks silky. Do not overbeat. Ganache will thicken as it cools. Keep at room temperature. You can make this ahead of time and keep in the refrigerator, but bring it to room temperature before serving.

☐ For a nice cake or pastry filling, combine Chocolate Ganache in a mixing bowl with ½ cup heavy cream. Beat until ganache thickens and forms soft peaks. Do not overbeat or it will become grainy. Or, for an elegant and delicious way to serve Chocolate Cake (recipe page 216), mix half of the Chocolate Ganache with ½ cup heavy cream, use this mixture as a filling, and reserve the other half for the cake's top. Let some of the ganache flow over the edges. It will have a silky sheen after it sits for a few minutes.

Chocolate with German Coconut Frosting

What sets this chocolate cake apart from others is that it is prepared with honey, not sugar. The German Coconut Frosting makes this cake irresistible!

CHOCOLATE CAKE

2½ ounces unsweetened chocolate
1¼ cups unbleached white flour
⅔ cup unsweetened cocoa powder
1½ teaspoons baking powder
1½ teaspoons baking soda
½ teaspoon salt
3 eggs, room temperature
1¼ cups honey
⅔ cup vegetable oil
2 teaspoons vanilla
¾ cup buttermilk, room temperature

☐ Melt chocolate in a double boiler. Set aside to cool.
☐ Preheat oven to 350°.
☐ Combine dry ingredients. Mix well with a fork or sift so that the cocoa is well incorporated with the flour (it tends to clump together).
☐ In a separate bowl, beat the eggs until they are light. Add honey and mix well. Add the oil and vanilla, and beat until combined.
☐ Add the buttermilk, a little at a time, to the cooled chocolate, stirring well after each addition.
☐ Add the buttermilk-chocolate mixture to the honey-egg mixture, beating well. Stir in the dry ingredients just until combined. Do not beat.
☐ Pour into 2 buttered and floured 9-inch cake pans. Bake at 350° for 30 to 35 minutes. Cake is done when a cake tester inserted in the middle comes out clean. Let cool before taking out of pans.
☐ Let cake cool completely before frosting.

GERMAN COCONUT FROSTING

½ cup butter
¼ cup maple syrup
½ cup honey
3 eggs
1 cup heavy cream
1 teaspoon vanilla extract
2⅓ cups unsweetened shredded coconut
1 cup chopped walnuts

☐ Combine butter, maple syrup, honey, eggs, and heavy cream in a heavy-bottomed saucepan. Cook over medium heat, stirring with a whisk until it begins to thicken. Remove from heat. Stir in vanilla, coconut, and walnuts.

☐ Cool to room temperature before filling and frosting cake.

☐ Makes enough to frost and fill one 9-inch, double-layer cake.

Cheesecake with Fresh Strawberry Glaze

Cheesecake is a dessert usually enjoyed by everyone, and it is a sure winner with children. This one is nice served plain, with the Fresh Strawberry Glaze, or simply with fresh berries on the side. Try the Pumpkin Cheesecake variation for a flavorful change.

We like to use whole wheat graham crackers when making the crust. Try them—you will notice a whole-grain flavor and a little less sweetness.

GRAHAM CRACKER CRUST

2 packages (½ pound) whole wheat graham crackers
6 tablespoons butter, melted
¼ cup honey
½ cup ground pecans (optional)

☐ Crush graham crackers into fine crumbs. A blender works well if you crush half of them at a time, or crush using a rolling pin on the counter. Add pecans, if desired, and mix well.
☐ Add butter and honey to crushed crackers, and mix well. Press crust into bottom and up the sides of an 8- or 9-inch springform pan.
☐ Prebake crust at 375° for 5 minutes.

CHEESECAKE

16 ounces cream cheese, softened
½ cup maple syrup or honey
1 cup sour cream
2 teaspoons vanilla
1 egg
2 tablespoons cornstarch or arrowroot
1 tablespoon lemon zest (optional)

☐ Beat cream cheese until smooth. Add honey or maple syrup, and beat until well combined. Add sour cream, vanilla, and egg. Blend together. Sprinkle cornstarch or arrowroot on mixture and beat in. Add lemon zest, if desired.

☐ Pour cheesecake mix into crust, and bake at 375° for 25 to 30 minutes, or until set. The middle may jiggle a little at first, but it will set up as it cools.

FRESH STRAWBERRY GLAZE

1 pint strawberries
½ tablespoon cornstarch or arrowroot
¼ cup cold water
¼ cup honey

☐ Clean and hull strawberries. Set aside a few of the nicest looking strawberries for the top of the cheesecake. Purée the rest to get 1 cup of strawberry purée.
☐ Dissolve cornstarch or arrowroot in cold water.
☐ In a saucepan, combine strawberry purée and honey. Bring to a boil. Slowly stir in cornstarch dissolved in water, stirring constantly. Continue to stir, and bring to a boil. Remove from the heat at once.
☐ Decorate the top of the cheesecake with the strawberries reserved from the glaze. While the topping and the cake are still warm, pour the topping over berries, glazing the cheesecake and berries.
☐ Refrigerate until set, at least 2 to 3 hours.

VARIATION: PUMPKIN CHEESECAKE

Use honey, and substitute 1½ cups of fresh or canned pumpkin purée for the sour cream. Use 2 eggs and add ½ teaspoon each of ginger, cinnamon, and nutmeg. It's great with the ground pecans added to the crust.

Rhubarb-Walnut

This is a very versatile cake recipe. Use peeled and diced apples instead of rhubarb, or use part apples and part rhubarb. It is great without a frosting, or serve it with a little whipped cream or ice cream. It's delicious for brunch or tea as well as a dessert.

½ cup butter
1 cup honey
2 eggs, beaten
1 teaspoon vanilla
½ cup plain yogurt
2 cups flour (all unbleached white flour, or 1 cup whole
    wheat pastry flour and 1 cup unbleached white flour)
½ teaspoon salt
2 teaspoons baking soda
1 teaspoon cinnamon
½ teaspoon allspice
3 cups chopped rhubarb
½ cup chopped walnuts

☐ Preheat oven to 350°.
☐ Cream butter. Add honey to butter, and beat until creamy. Add eggs, vanilla, and yogurt. Beat until well blended.
☐ Combine dry ingredients in a separate bowl. Stir into wet ingredients until well-mixed.
☐ Stir in rhubarb and walnuts.
☐ Butter and flour a 13 x 9-inch cake pan or two 9-inch cake pans.
☐ Bake cake for 30 to 35 minutes. Cake is done when a cake tester inserted in the middle comes out clean.

Maple-Rum-Pecan Cheesecake

Here is a cheesecake sweetened with maple syrup. The addition of pecans changes the usual creamy texture we associate with cheesecake. Maple-Rum-Pecan Cheesecake is sure to satisfy cravings for a rich dessert.

1 prebaked Graham Cracker Crust (recipe on page 218)
24 ounces cream cheese
½ cup maple syrup
2 tablespoons cornstarch or arrowroot
⅓ cup whipping cream or half and half
1 egg
3 tablespoons dark rum
¾ cup pecans, coarsely chopped

☐ Preheat oven to 375°.
☐ Beat cream cheese until creamy. Add maple syrup, and beat until no lumps of cream cheese remain.
☐ Dissolve cornstarch or arrowroot in whipping cream or half and half.
☐ Add cream with cornstarch, egg, and rum to cream cheese mixture. Combine well.
☐ Stir in pecans. Pour into prepared crust.
☐ Bake for 40 to 45 minutes.
☐ Cheesecake may jiggle a little in the middle but will set up as it cools. It may brown slightly around the edges, but it should not be completely brown.

Chocolate Carrot with Chocolate Cream Cheese Frosting

Chocolate Carrot Cake is a rich, moist cake with a hint of cinnamon and carrots. Frost it with Chocolate Ganache (page 214) or Chocolate Cream Cheese Frosting.

CHOCOLATE CARROT CAKE

2½ ounces unsweetened chocolate
1⅓ cups unbleached white flour
⅔ cup unsweetened cocoa powder
1½ teaspoons baking powder
1½ teaspoons baking soda
½ teaspoon salt
1 teaspoon ground cinnamon
3 eggs, room temperature
1¼ cups honey
⅔ cup vegetable oil
2 teaspoons vanilla extract
finely grated zest of 1 lemon
¾ cup buttermilk, room temperature
1½ cups grated carrots

☐ It is best to have all ingredients at room temperature. Chocolate tends to harden when it is mixed with cold milk or eggs.
☐ Preheat oven to 350°.
☐ Melt chocolate in a double boiler, and set it aside to cool.
☐ In a bowl, combine the flour, cocoa, baking powder, baking soda, salt, and cinnamon.

☐ In a separate bowl, beat eggs. Add honey, and beat until light. Add oil to eggs and beat. Stir in the vanilla and lemon zest. Add cooled chocolate and mix well. Stir in buttermilk.
☐ Stir in dry ingredients, just until combined. Stir in grated carrots.
☐ Pour batter into two 9-inch buttered and floured cake pans. Bake for 35 to 40 minutes, or until a cake tester inserted in the center comes out clean. Let cool before taking out of pans.
☐ Let cakes cool completely before frosting.

CHOCOLATE CREAM CHEESE FROSTING

This is a very rich frosting. Use it with the Chocolate Carrot Cake, Mocha Spice Cake (page 226), or Chocolate Cake (page 216).

½ cup butter, room temperature
1½ cups Neufchâtel, softened
¾ cup honey or maple syrup
¾ cup unsweetened cocoa powder
2 tablespoons Cafix™ (a coffee substitute made from grain) or instant coffee
1 tablespoon Grand Marnier™, rum, or crème de cacao

☐ Beat butter. Add the cream cheese, and beat until very smooth and creamy. Add the honey or syrup, and beat again. Add cocoa, Cafix™ or coffee, and liquor. Beat until well combined.
☐ Makes enough to fill and frost one 9-inch double-layer cake.

Poppyseed with Lemon Cream Frosting

The texture and nutty flavor of our Poppyseed Cake is delicious, especially when it is topped with our Lemon Cream Frosting. It's good for birthdays and other festive occasions.

POPPYSEED CAKE

⅔ cup milk
½ cup poppyseeds
½ cup butter
⅓ cup honey
½ cup maple syrup
4 eggs, separated, plus 1 additional egg white
2 teaspoons vanilla extract
2 cups unbleached white flour
4 teaspoons baking powder
¼ teaspoon salt

☐ Scald milk, removing from heat just before it boils. Add poppyseeds to milk, letting them soak until the milk is cool.

☐ Preheat oven to 350°.

☐ Cream butter. Beat in honey and maple syrup. Add the 4 egg yolks and beat again. Add vanilla and cooled milk.

☐ In a separate bowl, combine flour, baking powder, and salt. Stir dry ingredients into liquids just until combined.

☐ Beat the 5 egg whites until stiff but not dry. Gently fold them into cake batter.

☐ Butter and flour two 9-inch cake pans. Divide batter evenly between the pans. Bake for 20 to 25 minutes. Cake is done when center springs back when touched gently or when a cake tester comes out clean. Cool before taking out of the pan.

☐ Frost and layer with Lemon Cream Frosting (or use Lemon Cream between the layers and whipped cream frosting on top).

LEMON CREAM FROSTING

zest of ½ lemon
juice of 1 to 2 lemons (⅓ cup total)
½ cup water
2 tablespoons cornstarch or arrowroot
2 to 3 tablespoons honey
1½ cups heavy cream

☐ Combine lemon zest, lemon juice, water, and cornstarch or arrowroot in a small saucepan. Stir well to dissolve the cornstarch.

☐ Cook over medium heat, stirring constantly with a whisk, until thick.

☐ Remove from heat and stir in honey, tasting to determine how much honey is needed. It should be slightly tart. Cool completely.

☐ Pour frosting into a large mixing bowl. Add ¾ cup of the cream. Beat on medium speed until blended and creamy. Add remaining ¾ cup cream and continue beating until cream is thick and stiff. Immediately spread on cake and refrigerate until serving time.

☐ Makes enough to fill and frost one 9-inch double-layer cake.

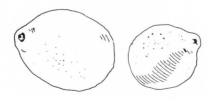

Mocha Spice

Mocha Spice Cake is a spicy chocolate cake that is tender and moist. It's simple and elegant when filled and frosted with sweetened whipped cream. Garnish with chocolate curls or chocolate-covered coffee beans.

You can also cut the recipe in half, and bake it in a 9-inch cake pan. Cut the cake into wedges, and serve it with a dollop of whipped cream and sliced strawberries.

2 ounces unsweetened chocolate
2 tablespoons instant coffee
⅓ cup water
1½ cups unbleached white flour
1 teaspoon baking soda
1 teaspoon cinnamon
1 teaspoon nutmeg
½ teaspoon baking powder
½ teaspoon salt
1 cup plain yogurt
½ teaspoon vanilla
½ cup soft butter
1 cup honey, warmed
2 eggs

☐ Melt chocolate in a double boiler, and set it aside to cool.
☐ Preheat oven to 350°.

☐ Dissolve coffee in water.

☐ Combine dry ingredients in a small bowl, and set aside.

☐ In a separate bowl, combine yogurt, coffee, and vanilla, and set aside.

☐ In another bowl, beat butter and honey together until creamy. Beat in eggs. Add cooled chocolate, and beat until blended.

☐ Add dry ingredients and yogurt mixture to butter mixture in small amounts, alternating the dry ingredients with the yogurt mixture. Stir until all is just well blended. Do not beat.

☐ Butter and flour two 8- or 9-inch cake pans, and pour the batter into them.

☐ Bake for 30 to 35 minutes. Cake is done when a cake tester inserted in the center comes out clean and dry. Let cool before taking out of pans.

☐ Let cakes cool completely before frosting.

Pie Dough

Use this recipe for one 8-inch or 9-inch, double-crust pie. For a single-crust pie, divide this recipe in half or make 2 crusts and freeze 1 shell for later.

> 2 cups flour (all unbleached white, or part white and part
>   whole wheat pastry flour)
> 1 teaspoon salt (omit if you are using salted butter or
>   margarine)
> ⅔ cup cold, unsalted butter
> 6 to 7 tablespoons cold water

> or

> 2 cups flour
> 1 teaspoon salt (omit if you are using salted butter or
>   margarine)
> 2 tablespoons vegetable shortening
> 8 tablespoons cold, unsalted butter
> 6 to 7 tablespoons cold water

☐ Combine flour and salt in a bowl. Cut the butter into small pieces, and add to the flour. With a pastry blender or with 2 knives, cut the butter (or shortening) into the flour until the mixture resembles coarse meal.

☐ Add the water 1 tablespoon at a time, mixing with a fork. Add only enough water to hold the dough together in a slightly moist ball. Divide the dough in half, forming 2 balls of dough. Wrap the dough well in plastic wrap. Chill for at least ½ hour.

☐ To roll the dough, sprinkle the work surface with a little flour. Flatten 1 dough ball with the palm of your hand and flour both sides. If the dough is too hard to work with, let it sit at room temperature for a while.

☐ Roll the dough from the middle to the edge in all directions, turning the dough as you roll to loosen it from the work surface and to make rolling easier. Continue rolling and turning until the dough is approximately 9 to 10 inches in diameter and ⅛ inch thick. Do not stretch the dough to fit the pan.

☐ Gently lay the pastry dough in the pie pan and press it in the pan without pulling or stretching. For a single-crust pie, leave about a half inch of extra dough along the edge. Turn the extra dough under, making a thicker edge. Flute the edge with your fingers.

☐ For a double-crust pie, lay the dough in the pie pan, and trim the excess dough so it is even with the pan. Roll out the second crust, and lay it to cover the filling. Trim the crust, leaving about 1 inch of extra dough. Fold this under the bottom crust to form a seal. Flute the edge. Slit the top crust to allow steam to escape.

☐ To prebake the pie crust: Form the shell in the pie pan, and chill it until it is firm. Press a piece of aluminum foil into the pie pan, forming it up the sides as well. Fill the foil with dried beans, rice, or aluminum pellets. This will keep the sides from shrinking down and the bottom from bubbling.

☐ Bake the pie shell in a preheated 400° oven for 20 minutes. Then, remove the foil and weights and return the shell to the oven to bake for 15 minutes until the shell is golden brown. The timing will depend on how thick the shell is. Check it often to be sure it does not overbake.

Apple-Cranberry

This is a very pretty pie. The tart cranberries go well with the sweet apples and honey. Try Apple-Cranberry Pie a la mode with a little cinnamon ice cream, and relax!

> *pastry for a 9-inch, double-crust pie, unbaked (recipe on page 228)*
> *2 tablespoons cornstarch or arrowroot*
> *3 tablespoons cold water*
> *2 cups cranberries (fresh or frozen, cleaned)*
> *½ cup honey*
> *4 medium-sized tart apples, peeled, cored, and sliced*
> *1 tablespoon freshly squeezed lemon juice*

☐ Make pastry dough.

☐ Dissolve the cornstarch or arrowroot in the cold water.

☐ In a saucepan, combine cranberries, honey, and apples. Bring the mixture to a boil, and then reduce the heat to a simmer. Simmer, stirring occasionally, for 4 to 5 minutes or until cranberries begin to pop.

☐ Stir the cornstarch mixture into the cranberry-apple mixture and simmer, stirring for 1 minute or until it begins to thicken. Transfer to a bowl and let it cool.

☐ Preheat oven to 425°.

☐ Roll out the bottom crust. Line a 9-inch pie pan with the prepared dough, cutting off any dough extending beyond the edge of the pie pan. Pour the cooled filling into pie shell.

☐ Roll out top crust and lay it over the fruit. Cut the dough, leaving a ½-inch overhang. Take the top crust and fold it under the bottom crust, pressing them together to form a seal. After the crust is folded under, flute the edge with your fingers or press the edge with a fork. Slit the top crust with a knife to allow steam to escape.

☐ Bake for 20 minutes, and then reduce the temperature to 350°, and bake for an additional 20 minutes.

☐ Let cool before serving.

Concord Grape

Seedless green and red grapes are often used in fresh fruit tarts, but Concord grapes make excellent pies. Serve pie warm or cold.

> pastry for a 9-inch, double-crust pie, unbaked (recipe on page 228)
> 6 cups Concord grapes
> ½ cup honey
> ½ teaspoon finely grated lime rind
> 1½ teaspoons fresh lime juice
> 1 tablespoon quick-cooking tapioca

☐ Make pastry dough. Roll out bottom shell, and line a 9-inch pie pan with the bottom crust. Refrigerate the other half of the dough until later.

☐ Wash grapes well. Slip off the grape skins by gently squeezing the grapes. Reserve the skins.

☐ In a saucepan, cook the grape pulp for 5 minutes over medium heat, stirring constantly. Remove the mixture from heat, and, to remove the seeds, force the grape pulp through a fine sieve into a bowl.

☐ Preheat oven to 450°.

☐ Add the grape skins, honey, lime rind, and juice to the grape pulp. Stir to combine.

☐ Sprinkle the tapioca on the pie shell, and pour the grape mixture into the shell.

☐ Roll out remaining dough, and lay it on top of the pie. Crimp edges. Slit the top crust to make air vents.

☐ Bake pie for 15 minutes. Reduce heat to 375°, and bake an additional 30 minutes.

☐ Pie will be very juicy and loose, but it firms up as it cools.

Peach

Nothing is as succulent as a juicy peach pie. It is great on its own, or try it with a scoop of vanilla ice cream. Serve warm or at room temperature.

> pastry for a 9-inch, double-crust pie, unbaked (recipe on page
>   228)
> 5 cups peaches, peeled and sliced (about 9 peaches)
> 1 tablespoon lemon juice
> 2 tablespoons flour
> ½ cup honey
> ¼ teaspoon salt
> 1 egg

☐ Prepare pastry dough. Line a 9-inch pie pan with the bottom crust. Refrigerate remaining dough while preparing pie.

☐ Peel peaches: Bring a pot of water to boil. Drop peaches into boiling water for 2 minutes. Remove peaches with a slotted spoon, and plunge them into a bowl of ice water. Skin will easily peel away from peach.

☐ Slice peaches into ½-inch thick slices, and drain the peach slices in a colander.

☐ Combine lemon juice, flour, honey, salt, and egg. Stir until well blended.

☐ Arrange peaches in the prepared pie shell, and pour honey mixture over them. Cover with the top pastry. Trim the edges, crimp them together, and cut steam vents.

☐ Bake at 450° for 15 minutes, reduce heat to 350°, and bake 25 minutes longer, until crust is done and peaches are tender. Cool on a rack.

VARIATION: PEACH PECAN

> 1 cup chopped, roasted pecans (see roasting instructions on
>   page 21)
> 2 tablespoons maple syrup or honey
> ½ teaspoon nutmeg

☐ Combine pecans, syrup or honey, and nutmeg, and spread on bottom crust before filling with peaches.

Strawberry-Rhubarb

Strawberry-Rhubarb Pie is a simple pie for your first summer barbecue. This is a juicy pie, full of flavor and color.

> *pastry for an 8- or 9-inch, double-crust pie, unbaked (see*
> *recipe on page 228)*
> *3 cups chopped rhubarb*
> *2 cups strawberries*
> *3 tablespoons cornstarch or arrowroot*
> *⅔ cup honey*

☐ Preheat oven to 450°.

☐ Clean rhubarb, and cut it into ½- to ¾-inch pieces. Clean strawberries, and cut into quarters.

☐ Combine fruit in a large bowl. Sprinkle cornstarch or arrowroot over the fruit. Stir gently. Add honey, and stir until well mixed.

☐ Prepare bottom pie shell. Pour fruit into the pie shell. Trim the dough so it is even with the sides of the pie pan. Roll out the remaining dough, and lay across the top of the fruit. Leave about 1 inch of dough to fold under the bottom crust, and trim the rest. Fold the top dough under the bottom, and press to seal. Crimp the edge and slit the top crust.

☐ Bake in a preheated 450° oven for 15 minutes. Reduce the temperature to 350°, and bake it for an additional 30 to 35 minutes. Pie will become firm as it cools. Serve at room temperature.

Sweet Potato–Pecan

This is a cross between a sweet potato pie and a pecan pie, a specialty of the South, where it is usually served with Chantilly cream. Our version is not quite as sweet but is very flavorful.

pastry for an 8- or 9-inch, double-crust pie, unbaked (recipe on page 228)

☐ Make pastry shell, and refrigerate it while preparing filling.

PECAN PIE SYRUP

1½ tablespoons butter, melted
2 eggs
½ cup honey
½ cup maple syrup
1 teaspoon vanilla
pinch salt
1 cup coarsely chopped pecans

☐ Melt butter. Combine it with the rest of ingredients except pecans. Mix well, then stir in pecans.

SWEET POTATO FILLING

> *1 cup sweet potato pulp (1 large or 2 small baked and peeled*
> *sweet potatoes)*
> *⅓ cup honey*
> *1 egg*
> *1 tablespoon unsalted butter*
> *1 tablespoon vanilla extract*
> *¼ teaspoon salt*
> *½ teaspoon ground cinnamon*
> *¼ teaspoon nutmeg*

☐ Combine all ingredients, and beat until smooth.
☐ Spoon sweet potato filling into pie crust. Pour Pecan Pie Syrup on top.
☐ Bake in a preheated 350° oven until a knife inserted in center comes out clean, about 1 hour and 20 to 30 minutes. Cool, and serve with whipped cream.

Blueberry

This is an easy, very flavorful pie. It is best made with fresh berries, but you can use frozen berries. For a great strawberry pie, make this recipe with fresh strawberries instead of blueberries. It's very refreshing!

> *pastry for a 9-inch, single-crust pie, baked and cooled (recipe*
> *for dough on page 228)*
> *4 cups blueberries (2 pints)*
> *⅓ cup honey*
> *¼ cup water*
> *2 tablespoons cornstarch or arrowroot*
> *2 tablespoons lemon juice*

☐ Clean blueberries, and divide in half. Set 2 cups aside.

☐ Combine 2 cups berries, honey, water, cornstarch or arrowroot, and lemon juice in a saucepan, and stir well. Cook over medium heat, stirring frequently until thickened, approximately 10 minutes. Remove from heat. While mixture is still hot, stir in the remaining 2 cups blueberries. Cool.

☐ When both shell and fruit mixture are cooled, spoon berries into pie shell. Refrigerate until serving time. Pie will set up as it chills.

☐ Cover pie with sweetened whipped cream, or slice and serve with a dollop of cream on each slice.

Tart Dough

1½ cups unbleached white flour
¼ teaspoon salt
6 tablespoons cold unsalted butter
1 egg
1 teaspoon lemon juice (optional)
1 to 2 tablespoons ice water

☐ Combine flour and salt in a bowl. Cut the butter into small pieces, and drop into the flour. Work the butter into the flour with a pastry blender or 2 knives until it resembles coarse meal.

☐ In a small bowl, lightly beat the egg. Add the lemon juice and water, and stir to combine. Slowly pour the liquid into the flour mixture while stirring with a fork. The mixture should be moist but not wet; it should hold together in a ball. Wrap the dough in plastic and refrigerate for 1 hour or more.

☐ To roll the dough, prepare a floured work surface. Flatten the dough with the palm of your hand. Lightly flour both sides of the dough. Roll out the dough from the center, moving toward the edges. Turn and flour the dough as you go to prevent it from sticking. Roll Tart Dough ⅛ inch thick.

☐ Carefully lay the dough in the tart pan. Trim the excess dough, leaving about 1 extra inch around the edge. Fold over the extra dough and press it against the sides to double the thickness of the sides.

□ Chill the tart shell for at least 1 hour before prebaking or filling.

□ To partially bake a tart shell, preheat oven to 425°. Line the shell with aluminum foil and fill with dried beans, rice, or aluminum pellets. This keeps the sides from caving in and the bottom from bubbling up.

□ Place the tart pan on the bottom shelf of the oven and bake for 15 minutes. Remove the pan from the oven, remove the weights, and return the shell to the oven for 5 minutes more to dry the bottom crust.

□ To bake a shell completely, follow the above steps, but bake for 20 minutes before removing the weights. Return the shell to the oven for an additional 5 minutes. The crust should be a light golden brown.

Sweet Tart Dough

This unique, Sweet Tart Dough resembles a shortbread. It works very well for the Banana–Coconut Cream Tart (page 244). Try it with other soft fruits, such as strawberries, nectarines, or kiwi, using a Pastry Cream base.

This recipe makes enough dough for two 9-inch tarts. If you are making only 1 tart, freeze the extra dough in a plastic bag. Bring it to room temperature when you are ready to use it, and press it into a tart pan.

⅔ cup unsalted butter, room temperature
1 cup date sugar
⅓ cup maple syrup
1 egg
1 teaspoon salt
¼ teaspoon cinnamon
½ cup finely ground pecans or walnuts
½ cup whole wheat pastry flour
1½ cups unbleached white flour

☐ Combine butter, date sugar, and maple syrup, stirring until well mixed. Stir in egg. Add the remaining ingredients. Stir until all is well mixed.

☐ Divide dough into 2 equal portions. Line a 9-inch tart pan with half of the dough: Flatten the dough and place in the center of the tart pan. Press the dough outwards until it covers the bottom and sides of the pan.

☐ Bake the shell on the bottom shelf of a preheated 375° oven for 15 to 20 minutes. After 10 minutes, check dough: You may need to poke holes in it with a fork to deflate air pockets, and you may need to rotate it on the shelf for even browning. Tart shell will be golden brown when done. If it is not completely done, the shell will get soggy from the filling. Cool before filling.

Pastry Cream

3 egg yolks
1½ tablespoons cornstarch or arrowroot
1½ tablespoons honey
¾ cup whole milk or half and half
1 tablespoon butter
¼ teaspoon vanilla

☐ Beat the egg yolks with the cornstarch or arrowroot and honey in a heavy bottomed saucepan.

☐ In another saucepan, bring the milk or half and half to a boil. Pour hot milk over yolks, whisking constantly until smooth. Cook slowly over low heat, stirring constantly until thickened.

☐ Stir in butter and vanilla. Let it cool. Stir occasionally while it is cooling so a skin does not form on top. Cover with a piece of wax paper and refrigerate until needed.

☐ Makes 1 cup.

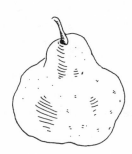

Fresh Fruit with Almond Pastry Cream

Fresh fruit tarts are beautiful and delicious, and the varieties are endless. They can be as simple as glazed and layered fresh fruit, or they can be an artful arrangement of many fruits. Try this with any of the fruits we have listed; we use them all, depending on what is in season.

> 1 partially baked, 9-inch Tart Dough (recipe on page 237)
> 1 recipe Almond Pastry Cream
> 3 or 4 medium pears, peaches, or nectarines, or 7 large
>   plums, cut into slices
> Fruit Glaze (recipe on page 242)

☐ Cover the bottom of the partially baked shell with Almond Pastry Cream. Arrange the fruit in the shell. It works well and looks nice to place fruit slices in a circular fashion, starting in the middle and working your way to the outer edge.

☐ Bake tart in a preheated 350° oven for 30 to 35 minutes. Tart is done when the filling is golden in spots and is set, not loose. While the tart is still hot, spoon or carefully brush glaze over the tart, completely covering the top. Serve at room temperature or chilled.

ALMOND PASTRY CREAM

> 2½ tablespoons butter, softened
> ½ cup finely ground almonds
> 2 tablespoons honey
> 1 egg
> 1 tablespoon cornstarch or arrowroot
> 1 teaspoon rum
> ⅓ cup Pastry Cream (recipe on page 240)

☐ Prepare the Pastry Cream at least 1 hour in advance of making the Almond Pastry Cream.
☐ Beat butter, and add the remaining ingredients except the Pastry Cream. Blend together until smooth. Add the Pastry Cream bit by bit until all of it is incorporated.

Almond-Hazelnut with Fruit Glaze

We like the almond-hazelnut combination. The hazelnuts add a little depth to the delicate almond flavor, making a sophisticated, flavorful tart. The simple Fruit Glaze complements its rich texture.

ALMOND-HAZELNUT TART

> 1 partially baked, 9-inch Tart Dough (recipe on page 237)
> ½ cup finely ground roasted almonds
> ½ cup finely ground roasted hazelnuts
> ½ cup butter
> ⅓ cup honey
> 2 eggs
> ¼ teaspoon almond extract
> 1 teaspoon grated lemon rind
> ¾ tablespoon flour
> apricot or orange glaze (see instructions in Fruit Glaze, below)
> sliced almonds or hazelnuts for garnish

☐ Spread almonds and hazelnuts on a cookie sheet, and roast in a 350° oven for 5 minutes or until just slightly browned. Let cool before grinding.
☐ Increase oven temperature to 400°.
☐ In a mixing bowl, beat butter. Add honey, and beat until creamy. Add eggs, and mix. Add almond extract, lemon rind, ground nuts, and flour. Mix until blended.
☐ Pour into a partially baked tart shell.
☐ Bake for 25 minutes. Test with cake tester. The tart is done when the tester comes out dry.
☐ Remove tart from oven, and glaze the tart while it is still warm. Sprinkle with sliced almonds or hazelnuts.

FRUIT GLAZE

Apricot, orange, and currant glazes are the most common glazes used and are the easiest to prepare. We like to use the currant glaze for tarts made with darker fruits such as cherries or berries. The apricot and orange are lighter glazes that can top nut tarts or those made with apricots, peaches, or bananas.

☐ Use jam or jelly to make a glaze. A 12-ounce jar makes more than you need for a 9-inch tart, but the glaze keeps for months in the refrigerator.

☐ Empty the jar of jam or jelly into a small saucepan. Bring to a boil over medium heat.

☐ Apricot jam and orange marmalade are best pressed through a fine sieve to strain out pieces of fruit. We find this easier to do after the jam has been heated.

☐ Add 2 tablespoons brandy or liqueur and 2 tablespoons apple juice or water to the sieved jam. Return to the heat and bring to a boil, stirring constantly.

☐ Currant jelly need not be sieved, so simply heat it to boiling and add brandy or a favorite fruit liqueur, and some water or juice to thin.

☐ Spoon or brush glaze over the tart filling while both the glaze and tart are hot.

Banana–Coconut Cream

Bananas and dried coconut are always available, so you can serve this tart year-round. It is a refreshing dessert during winter when our fresh fruit selection is limited. You can also make it with strawberries instead of the bananas.

Serve this tart the same day it is made. The crust gets soggy if it sits longer than a day, and the bananas tend to discolor.

> 1 baked, 9-inch Sweet Tart Dough (recipe on page 239)
> 1 cup Pastry Cream (recipe on page 240)
> ½ cup coconut, toasted
> 4 ripe bananas
> 1 cup heavy cream
> 2 tablespoons honey
> 1 teaspoon vanilla

☐ To toast the coconut, spread a single layer on a baking sheet and put in a 350° oven. Watch the coconut carefully, because it does not take long to toast. Remove from the oven when the coconut just begins to turn brown at the tips, approximately 5 minutes.

☐ Make Pastry Cream. Add coconut (reserving a couple of tablespoons to decorate the top) to the warm Pastry Cream. Then allow to cool completely before using. Fill cooled tart shell with Pastry Cream.

☐ Chop bananas into ¼- to ½-inch slices, and arrange slices over filling. Chill the tart while whipping cream.

☐ Beat heavy cream, honey, and vanilla until thick. Spread over bananas. Decorate top with toasted coconut.

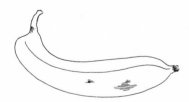

Cranberry-Orange-Walnut

This is certainly a festive tart for Thanksgiving or holiday entertaining. It is very colorful, sweet, and nutty.

Cranberry-Orange-Walnut is a very simple tart to make. If you have a tart shell already prepared, you can throw it together in just a few minutes.

> 1 partially baked, 9-inch Tart Dough (recipe on page 237)
> 2 large eggs
> ½ cup honey
> ¼ cup butter, melted and cooled
> 2 tablespoons orange juice
> 1 teaspoon vanilla
> ¼ teaspoon salt
> 1 cup chopped, cleaned cranberries
> ½ cup chopped walnuts
> 1½ teaspoons grated orange rind

☐ Preheat oven to 350°.
☐ Combine eggs, honey, butter, orange juice, vanilla, and salt. Beat with a whisk until smooth. Stir in cranberries, walnuts, and orange rind.
☐ Pour the filling into the prepared tart shell. Bake in the center of the oven for 40 to 45 minutes or until golden. Let cool completely on a rack.

Sliced Almond

This is a simple and elegant tart. The almond filling caramelizes as it cooks, creating a golden sheen that looks great with fresh berries and whipped cream. For an extra special treat, drizzle semisweet chocolate across the top.

1 partially baked, 9-inch Tart Dough (recipe on page 237)
1 cup sliced almonds
1 cup heavy cream
⅓ cup maple syrup
¼ cup honey
⅛ teaspoon salt
1 tablespoon kirsch
1 tablespoon Grand Marnier™
2 drops almond extract

☐ Combine ingredients in a heavy saucepan. Cook over medium heat, stirring frequently, until mixture thickens and becomes golden brown, approximately 20 minutes.

☐ Pour into prepared tart shell. Bake at 350° for 50 minutes to 1 hour. Filling will bubble and rise slightly in pan and then settle.

☐ Tart is done when filling has caramelized and turned a deep golden brown. Cool completely before serving.

☐ Serve with a dollop of whipped cream, or fill a pastry bag with whipped cream and pipe cream around the edge of the tart.

Pecan

This is a classic tart, sweetened with maple syrup and honey. This is a great alternative to pecan pie at Thanksgiving. For chocolate lovers, add ½ cup chocolate chips when you add the chopped nuts.

1 partially baked, 9-inch Tart Dough (recipe on page 237)
3 tablespoons butter
1½ cups pecan halves
2 eggs
¼ cup maple syrup
½ cup honey
1¼ teaspoons vanilla
⅛ teaspoon salt

☐ Preheat oven to 350°.
☐ Melt butter and set aside to cool.
☐ Coarsely chop 1 cup of the nuts. Reserve ½ cup nuts to decorate the top of the tart.
☐ Beat eggs. Add maple syrup, honey, vanilla, salt, and cooled butter. Beat until smooth. Stir in chopped nuts.
☐ Pour mixture into partially baked shell. Arrange pecan halves on top.
☐ Bake for 30 to 35 minutes or until just set, not dry.

Fruit Crisp

Crisps have always been a popular fruit dessert at the restaurant. Our topping includes ground nuts and oats, which gives it a nice crunchy texture. We often combine different fruits, like pears and apples or cherries and apricots, which adds variety and gives delicious results. Of course, a plain apple crisp is always good and can be varied with raisins or coconut.

You can make this recipe with vegetable oil in place of the butter for a non-dairy dessert. We have given quantities for a 9 x 9-inch pan, but if you would like to use a 9 x 13-inch pan, just double the recipe.

½ cup ground roasted nuts: walnuts or almonds
2 cups rolled oats
⅓ cup whole wheat pastry flour
dash salt
½ teaspoon cinnamon
6 cups fruit—apples, pears, nectarines, apricots, or cherries
raisins, coconut, or additional nuts (optional)
1 teaspoon cornstarch or arrowroot
⅓ cup apple juice
¼ cup honey or maple syrup
⅓ cup butter, melted

☐ Roast nuts in a 350° oven until golden (about 10 minutes). Let nuts cool. Grind in a food grinder or a food processor.

☐ Spread the oats on a cookie sheet and roast them in a 350° oven for 10 minutes. Let oats cool. Divide the oats in half. Grind half of the oats to a fine powder in a food grinder or food processor.

☐ Keep oven heated at 350°.

☐ Combine all of the oats with nuts, flour, salt, and cinnamon.

☐ Prepare the fruit. Wash, peel, and cut it into slices. Place fruit in the bottom of an 8-inch or 9-inch square baking dish. Add optional ingredients if desired.

☐ Dissolve cornstarch or arrowroot in 2 tablespoons of the juice. Pour remaining juice into a saucepan, and cook over medium heat. When juice is hot, stir in cornstarch mixture. Stir constantly until the juice thickens. Pour the thickened juice over the fruit in the baking dish.

☐ Combine honey or syrup and melted butter with the dry ingredients. Stir until well combined. The mixture will be wet and sticky. Take walnut-sized pieces of the topping in your fingers and distribute it evenly over the entire dish.

☐ Bake for 45 to 50 minutes. When it is done, the topping is golden brown and the fruit is soft. Serve warm or at room temperature. It is best eaten the same day it is made. Serves 9.

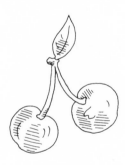

Apple-Blackberry Cobbler

Fresh berries, peaches, and nectarines all work equally well in this recipe. At the Cafe, we prepare cobbler in individual portions, baking them in custard cups with a round biscuit atop each one. Cobbler is best eaten the day it is prepared.

BISCUIT DOUGH

2 cups unbleached white flour
½ teaspoon salt
1 teaspoon baking powder
¼ teaspoon baking soda
4 tablespoons butter, chilled
½ cup plus 2 tablespoons buttermilk

☐ Put flour, salt, baking powder, and baking soda in a large bowl. Stir to combine. Add butter in chunks, and cut in with a pastry blender or 2 knives. When dough is crumbly, stir in buttermilk, and mix until dough holds together.

☐ Turn out dough onto a floured surface and knead 10 to 12 times, no more. Return to bowl and let it set while fruit is prepared.

FRUIT MIXTURE

3 cups blackberries
2 medium tart apples, peeled, cored, and sliced
1 tablespoon lemon juice
¼ cup honey

☐ Combine berries, apples, and lemon juice in a bowl.

☐ Place fruit mixture into an 8- or 9-inch baking dish. Drizzle honey over fruit.

☐ Roll biscuit dough ¼-inch thick and slightly smaller than the diameter of your baking dish.

☐ Lay dough on the top of the fruit, leaving room for the fruit to bubble up. Slice through the dough with a sharp knife to make steam vents.

☐ Bake in a preheated 450° oven for 20 to 25 minutes. Cobbler is done when the biscuit dough is brown and the fruit is tender. Set cobbler on a rack to cool for at least 15 minutes before serving.

☐ May be served warm or at room temperature. Serves 6 to 8.

Caramelized Apple Pastry

Our version of the classic Tart Tatin. This dessert is very impressive to serve to guests, and the pure maple syrup caramel is heavenly. We feel safe to say, "You'll have no leftovers." As an alternative to the homemade version, puff pastry is widely available in the frozen food sections of grocery stores.

PUFF PASTRY DOUGH

1 scant cup unbleached white flour
4 tablespoons butter, softened
½ teaspoon salt
3 tablespoons water
5 tablespoons cold butter

☐ Combine flour and 4 tablespoons softened butter in a bowl. Mix together with your hands until well combined.

☐ Dissolve salt in the water. Add water to the flour-butter mixture, and mix together just until it begins to hold together.

☐ Form the dough into a ball. Put the ball of dough in a small bowl, cover with plastic wrap or a damp towel, and refrigerate for 1 hour.

☐ Remove dough from the refrigerator. Place dough on a lightly floured work surface. Roll it out into a rectangle, about ¼ inch thick.

☐ Place the cold butter between 2 sheets of wax paper and tap it with a rolling pin to make it more pliable. Break the butter into small pieces and distribute the butter pieces over ⅔ of the dough. Fold the dough into thirds, folding width-wise, first turning the section that does not have butter on it.

☐ Turn the dough so the fold is perpendicular to you (the ends should be facing you), and roll out the dough to ½-inch thickness. Do not roll toward the fold! Reflour the dough or table lightly to keep the dough from sticking.

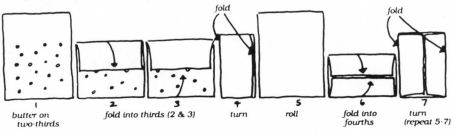

butter on   fold into thirds (2 & 3)   turn   roll   fold into   turn
two-thirds   fourths   (repeat 5-7)

☐ Fold the dough again. This time, fold in the ends width-wise so they touch in the middle; then, fold in half in the same direction to end up with fourths. Turn the dough so the folded edge is perpendicular to you (the ends should be facing you). Roll it out again to ½-inch thickness, and fold into fourths once again.

☐ Cover the dough well, and refrigerate for 1 hour.

☐ Roll the dough into a rectangle and fold into fourths a third time. Repeat once more. Wrap it well, and refrigerate for at least 1 more hour, or until you are ready to use it. Use this dough the same day you make it, but you may keep it at this stage until you are ready for it.

TART

1 recipe Puff Pastry Dough
4 to 5 large tart cooking apples, approximately 2½ pounds
½ cup water or apple juice
¾ cup heavy cream
½ cup maple syrup

☐ Preheat oven to 400°.

☐ Peel, core, and quarter apples. Poach in ½ cup water or apple juice for 5 to 8 minutes until apples have softened. A fork should pierce the apples easily, but the apples should not be mushy. Pour off the liquid.

☐ Bring heavy cream and maple syrup to a low boil over a moderate flame in a heavy-bottomed saucepan. Stir frequently until mixture thickens and begins to caramelize, which will take approximately 20 minutes. Make sure to let it boil and get very thick (it will reach 220° on a candy thermometer).

☐ Pour the caramel into a 10-inch round cake pan or baking dish. Tilt the pan completely, covering the bottom of the pan with the caramel. Lay the apples on top of the caramel, arranging them close together in a single layer.

☐ Roll out the dough into a 10-inch round. Prick the dough with a fork, and lay it over the apples.

☐ Bake for 5 minutes at 400°, and then increase the heat to 450°. Bake for 20 minutes more or until the pie crust looks done.

☐ Turn the dish over on a serving platter. Serve warm.

Gingerbread with Apple or Pear Sauce

A traditional American dessert. Gingerbread has always been a favorite at the Cafe, and it is always a winner with children. We like to pour a fruit sauce onto a dessert plate followed by a slice of Gingerbread and a dollop of whipped cream. It is very moist, making it a cake that keeps well. Serve it for brunch as well as for dessert.

1 cup butter, room temperature, or ½ cup butter and ½ cup
vegetable oil
1 cup honey
¾ cup dark molasses (not blackstrap)
¾ cup boiling water
3 large eggs
2¾ cups unbleached white flour
1 teaspoon salt
1½ teaspoons baking soda
1 teaspoon cinnamon
1 teaspoon ground ginger

☐ Cut butter into small pieces, and combine it with honey and molasses in a large mixing bowl. Pour boiling water into bowl, and stir until butter melts. Set aside to cool.
☐ Add eggs to cooled butter mixture. Beat well.
☐ In a separate bowl, combine dry ingredients. Stir into wet mixture, and beat until smooth.
☐ Pour batter into a buttered 9 x 13-inch pan or two 9-inch cake pans.
☐ Bake at 325° for 50 to 60 minutes. Test with a cake tester. It should come out clean.
☐ Serve with sweetened whipped cream or with Apple or Pear Sauce or puréed strawberries.

APPLE OR PEAR SAUCE

This recipe works well with either pears or apples, or a combination of both. Serve it with Gingerbread or Vegetable Pancakes (page 208).

> *4 medium apples or pears*
> *½ cup apple juice*
> *1 tablespoon honey*
> *¼ teaspoon cinnamon*
> *2 tablespoons lemon juice (optional)*
> *¼ cup white wine (optional)*

☐ Peel fruit. Core, and cut into chunks. Cook fruit in juice until very soft. Add honey, cinnamon, and lemon juice. Purée fruit mixture in a blender until smooth.

☐ If you are using wine, return the sauce to the saucepan, and add the wine. Simmer gently for 3 to 5 minutes.

☐ Serve warm or at room temperature.

☐ Makes 2 cups.

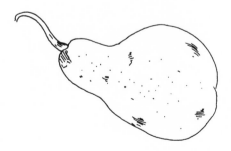

Maple Pot de Creme

The incomparable flavor of maple syrup baked in this classic custard is undeniably delicious. Maple Pot de Creme is definitely not a low-calorie, low-cholesterol dish! For those who can splurge, this seems to be the one dessert our customers cannot refuse.

2 cups heavy cream
½ cup whole milk
9 egg yolks
½ cup maple syrup
½ tablespoon vanilla extract

☐ Preheat oven to 350°.
☐ Place 6 custard cups into a shallow baking dish.
☐ Combine the cream and milk in a saucepan. Bring to a low boil over moderate heat. Remove from heat.
☐ In a separate bowl, gently whisk together the egg yolks, maple syrup, and vanilla. Avoid creating a froth.
☐ Gently whisk the cream into the egg yolk mixture 1 cup at a time. When well combined, pour into custard cups. Pour enough boiling water into the pan to surround the cups with 1 inch of water.
☐ Place pan in the center of oven. Bake for 45 minutes. Custards will be done when they are firm. Chill.

Rice Pudding

Rice Pudding is a delicious dessert and a great way to use up leftover rice. Children love it! There are endless variations: Try coconut milk or soy milk in place of the milk, sweet or white rice (use ½ cup less water), or vary the fruits, spices, and nuts.

1 cup brown rice
2½ cups water
¼ cup honey or maple syrup
½ tablespoon butter
¼ teaspoon salt
½ teaspoon cinnamon
⅓ cup finely ground nuts: almonds, walnuts, or hazelnuts
¾ cup chopped dates
¾ cup unsweetened coconut
1½ cups whole milk or half and half
1 egg
1 teaspoon vanilla extract
chopped apples, raisins, dried apricots (optional)

☐ Combine rice and water in a medium saucepan. Bring to a boil. Reduce heat and simmer, covered, until all water has been absorbed, approximately 45 minutes.

☐ Stir honey or maple syrup, butter, salt, cinnamon, nuts, dates, coconut, and milk or half and half into rice. Add optional fruit. Continue to cook over medium heat, stirring frequently. Cook until thick and creamy, about 15 minutes.

☐ Remove pudding from heat. Beat egg in a small bowl. Add a small amount of pudding to the egg and mix. Add a little more pudding, stirring until egg is warm. Stir egg mixture into pudding.

☐ Return to moderate flame and cook briefly. Stir until mixture thickens up again, approximately 5 minutes.

☐ Remove from heat. Add vanilla.

☐ Stir pudding as it cools to prevent a skin from forming on the top.

☐ Serve cold with a dollop of plain yogurt. Serves 6.

Apple-Sesame Kanten

Kanten is a traditional Asian fruit dessert. We like to make it into a creamy pudding and top it with nuts and fresh fruit. You can vary the juice used, making many different flavors. Apple juice with almond butter is a good combination; pineapple-coconut juice with sliced oranges is very refreshing. It's pretty served in goblets, and easy to layer 2 different flavors.

6 cups apple juice
2 sticks agar
½ cup tahini
fresh fruit for garnish

☐ Pour apple juice into a saucepan. Break agar sticks into pieces, and soften pieces in juice. When agar is soft, put saucepan over medium-high heat. Bring to a boil, then simmer for 15 minutes, stirring frequently, until agar dissolves.

☐ Pour juice mixture into a bowl, and refrigerate until kanten sets, approximately 1½ to 2 hours.

☐ Using a blender, blend kanten with tahini until smooth and creamy. If necessary, blend in batches, and then pour into individual serving dishes.

☐ Serve cold, and garnish with fresh fruit: berries, grapes, kiwi, or citrus. It's pretty served in stemmed glasses. Serves 8.

VARIATION

Use apple-peach or apple-cherry juice and use almond butter instead of tahini.

INDEX

262

croquettes with almonds and vegetables, 196; in croquettes with vegetables and pecans, 204; in pudding, 257

BUCKWHEAT; *flour, in scones,* 102; *groats (kasha), in croquettes,* 189

BUTTER; *clarifying,* 125

BUTTERCUP SQUASH; *see* SQUASH, WINTER

BUTTERMILK; *Scones,* 102; *Cornbread,* 107

BUTTERNUT SQUASH; *see* SQUASH, WINTER

BUTTERS; *Cranberry-Mint Beurre Blanc,* 119; *Ginger-Lime-Peanut Beurre Noisette,* 136; *Roasted Shallot–Garlic,* 140

CABBAGE; *Chinese, in soup with miso,* 60; *in Thai-style stew,* 161; *in Shepherd's Pie,* 182

CANTALOUPE(S); *in soup,* 49, 50

CARDAMOM; *Bread,* 96

CARROT(S); *in soba salad,* 23; *in soup with leeks, squash, parsnip, and potato,* 68; *in Chinese-Style Vegetables,* 120; *in Vegetable-Fish Stir-Fry,* 133; *in loaf with walnuts and cheese,* 152; *in chili with black beans,* 154; *in Thai-style stew,* 161; *in Vegetable Terrine,* 166; *in Winter Vegetable Pie,* 173; *in Vietnamese tempeh salad,* 178; *in*

Shepherd's Pie, 182; *in croquettes with chickpeas,* 190; *in croquettes with red beans and basmati rice,* 194; *in croquettes with brown rice and almonds,* 196; *in croquettes with tofu and peanuts,* 202; *in croquettes with wild rice and pecans,* 204; *in pancakes,* 208; *in cake with chocolate,* 222

CAULIFLOWER; *in stew with chickpeas,* 158

CELERY; *in chili with black beans,* 154; *in Shepherd's Pie,* 182; *in croquettes with chickpeas,* 190; *in croquettes with red beans and basmati rice,* 194; *in croquettes with brown rice and almonds,* 196; *in croquettes with tofu and peanuts,* 202; *in croquettes with wild rice and pecans,* 204

CHEDDAR; *in bread,* 79

CHEESE; *in quesadillas,* 32; *in loaf with carrots and walnuts,* 152; *in gratin with spinach, zucchini, and herbs,* 164; *in terrine with vegetables,* 166; *in croquettes with butternut squash and walnuts,* 200 *see also specific kinds of cheeses*

CHERRY(IES); *in soup with lemon,* 47; *in Fruit Crisp,* 248

CHEVRE; *rolled in hazelnuts,* 20

CHICKPEA(S), DRIED; *in soup with pumpkin,* 54; *in soup with vegetables,* 66; *in stew*

with vegetables, 158; *in pilaf with couscous,* 180; *in croquettes with vegetables,* 190 *see also* BEAN(S), DRIED GARBANZO

CHILI; *Black Bean–Vegetable,* 154

CHILIES; *see* PEPPER(S), CHILI

CHILI PASTE; *in dressing,* 22

CHOCOLATE; *Ganache,* 215; *Cake,* 216; *in cake with carrot,* 222; *in frosting with Neufchatel,* 223; *in cake with coffee,* 226

CHOWDER; *Corn,* 55

CHUTNEYS; *Apricot,* 123 *see also* RELISHES

CINNAMON; *Bread,* 82; *in cake with chocolate,* 226

COCONUT; *in bread with orange,* 104; *in homemade Coconut Milk,* 116; *in frosting,* 217; *in tart with banana,* 244; *in Fruit Crisp,* 248

COCONUT MILK; *in soup with lentils and sweet potato,* 57; *homemade,* 116; *in Caribbean Fish and Shrimp Stew,* 117; *used in rice,* 136; *in stew with chickpeas and vegetables,* 158; *in Thai-style Stock,* 160

COD; *in fish cakes,* 122

COFFEE; *instant, in cake,* 226

CONDIMENTS; *see* BUTTERS; MARINADES; SALAD DRESSINGS; VINAIGRETTES

BRENDA LANGTON opened Cafe Brenda in the heart of the Minneapolis warehouse district in 1986; it has received recognition as one of the finest restaurants in the country and as an innovator in gourmet vegetarian cuisine. Her first restaurant, Cafe Kardamena in Saint Paul, was a preeminent vegetarian restaurant in the Upper Midwest. Brenda also teaches cooking classes and is a consultant on natural foods and diet. She operates her restaurant and natural food business with her husband, Timothy Kane. They live in Minneapolis with their daughter, Celina.

MARGARET STUART was a pastry chef at Cafe Kardamena and is now active in several facets of the natural foods movement, from gardening to cooking. She has a bachelor's degree in horticulture and owns a garden design business in the Twin Cities.